FRIENDSHIP

Sisters for a Journey

Jessie Seneca

Three are even better,
for a triple-braided cord is not easily broken.
Ecclesiastes 4:12

Friendship

Sisters for a Journey

Jessie Seneca

Foreword by Gwen Smith, *Girlfriends in God*

FRIENDSHIP: *Sisters for a Journey*
Copyright © 2016 Jessie Seneca
ISBN 978-1-938796-03-6 (soft cover)
ISBN 978-1-938796-05-0 (eBook)
Library of Congress Control Number 2016942212

Edited by
Connie Rinehold and Melissa Peitsch

Cover Illustration by
Kely Vanek, Cassidy Communications, Inc.

Interior Design by
Candy Abbott

Published by
Fruitbearer Publishing LLC
P.O. Box 777, Georgetown, DE 19947
302.856.6649 • FAX 302.856.7742
www.fruitbearer.com • info@fruitbearer.com

Dedication

To my loving mother
Kathryn Eschenbach
and
In memory of my father
Carl Eschenbach

Where I first viewed the art of true friendship

Table of Contents

Acknowledgments

I t all began, one afternoon, around the kitchen table of my good friend, Nellisa. I stopped over for a cup of tea and sweet conversation. That right there is an understatement. She has seven kids ranging from two to twenty-four. But somehow we manage to fit in some girl time with each other.

We became friends many years ago while in Bible study and our children attended elementary school together. It seemed to be an instant friendship that has weathered through illness, heartache, laughter, and love. Did I mention laughter? Oh, we do that well with our husbands in tow. Not only are we friends, but we are family friends. And for some of you reading this book, you know that when our husbands mesh with our friend's husband, we've found a gift.

While watching little ones play under our feet and others sharing their newest art project, out of the blue, Nellisa says, "I think your next book should be on friendship!"

Let me just say, I was not thinking of my next writing project as I had only finished the Bible study, *Joseph: A Life of Rejection, Resilience and Respect* the week prior. For that matter, it was still with the editor.

"Because you are good at it," she said in her next breath.

That statement was enough to frighten me to death. "Good at it?" I said.

My thoughts started to swirl. Anything good in me is because of Jesus. At times, if she could hear the conversation in my head, she would not have said that.

If you are anything like me, you wish you would have been a better friend to that certain person—been more encouraging, less judgmental, or a better listener.

Time passed, but the words of my dear friend lasted.

Fast forward one year ~

I was on my daily walk with my golden-doodles, Bella and Murphy. The winter started to break and we were able to do our much loved trail. I still had boots on, but there was no ice to dodge. I don't know who was happier, me or the dogs. I love our walks.

I use our walks as my therapy time with God and much needed exercise for our furry friends.

A time to meet with Him in prayer.

A time to converse with Him about a decision.

A time to share my hurts.

A time to thank Him for who He is.

A time to ask questions.

A time to bring others before Him.

A time to soak in His majesty.

A time to listen.

As I listened, this particular early spring day, I felt a whisper in my spirit. A whisper that confirmed, it's time to write again. *Friendship.*

As soon as I returned home, this confirmation was meant to be a phone call. Not a text.

"Nellisa, you better get your prayers going. I am going to start that book you spoke over me."

I am so excited to walk with you through the seasons and styles of friendship. Sometimes it might look a little messy and other times glorious, but I know God will use it all to grow and stretch us. He will convict and confirm through the many Scriptures, stories, and steps we take to become a better friend, sister, mother, daughter, aunt, and grandmother. We are never beyond the age of learning more about one of the greatest gifts God has given us — *Friendship.*

I have many faces and memories at the forefront of my mind with the typing of every word, paragraph, and chapter. Please know I am not going to use the names of my actual friends except Nellisa — she is real. I do not want to miss anyone and lose a friend. HA!

Jessie

Friendship . . . is not something you learn in school. But if you haven't learned the meaning of friendship, you really haven't learned anything. ~ Muhammad Ali

Foreword

I'm gonna shoot straight here: shows like *The Big Bang Theory* and old reruns of *Friends, Gilmore Girls,* and *Sex and The City* have highlighted the importance of friendships, but they've led us in the wrong direction.

Friendships are my jam. Totally my thing. I love my besties and they love me back. I can think of five main ways we build into one another's lives: prayer, laughter, love, grace, and truth. I don't know of a time when empty conversations led by do-what-feels-good-to-you theology was ever helpful to me. Can you?

I cofounded a ministry team that comes alongside of women to encourage them toward Jesus. We "do life" together through devotions and conferences. We celebrate the importance of relationships and take seriously the calling God has on our lives, but we are not the bring-a-casserole-when-you-just-had-surgery kind of girlfriends. We are spiritual mentors.

We all need fleshy friends to do life with, not just electronic acquaintances on social media and not just spiritual mentors from books and the internet. We need relationships of substance: first with God, then with others. We need face to face, heart to heart, struggle to struggle sisters. We need trusted confidants who have the courage to tell us when we've spoken out of line, when we should be speaking up, when we are believing lies, being stubborn, or dripping with drama. And who will also tell us when we have red lipstick on our teeth. We need *real* friends with whom we can share wisdom, talk truth, wave pompoms, and cry salty tears. And if she can give a good foot rub, all the better!

When it comes to friendships, it is possible to flourish, even if your track record or current bounty seems fractured or scarce. This is a message I needed to understand on the playground as a little girl, and it is one I need to understand and grow in today — and that's what this book is all about.

Jessie has learned a lot about friendship over the years, and she's pulled up a comfy sister-chair to encourage you in yours. She doesn't write from a place of perfection, but from a heart of humility, honesty, wisdom, and sincere reflection.

If you are looking for a better understanding of what it looks like to have and to be a good friend, then this book will be a great companion to you on your journey.

If you are looking for relatable stories and biblical wisdom that will help deepen your current friendships, then look no further. You've found it.

It's an honor to introduce you to my friend, Jessie Seneca.

Gwen Smith
Friend to a band of beautifully broken chicks
Author of *I Want It All*
Cofounder of Girlfriends in God

Chapter One

A Girl's Best Friend

There is nothing more important than the love of God, and
the love of family and friends. ~ Robin Graham Scott

Remember the song, "Diamonds are a Girl's Best Friend," most famously performed by Marilyn Monroe in the 1953 film *Gentlemen Prefer Blondes*?

The end of the song goes like this, "Diamonds! Diamonds! I don't mean rhinestones!"

Regardless of your feelings toward the song, it does teach us a thing or two about relationships. We want the real thing and nothing short of it. We desire real, authentic, and meaningful relationships. The kind you treasure; the kind that energize your soul.

When we translate that desire to our heavenly relationship with God, we experience an unspeakable security, which overflows into our earthly ones.

After a diamond is painstakingly cut and shaped to perfectly bounce light, the final step in its completion is to carefully polish it to its final level of shine. We want the real thing, not the imitation, in our walk with our friends and in our relationships. We can be the polish that encourages others to be all God has called them to be or, if we lack the polish, we can be one who tarnishes another's walk.

My hope through this book is that you will come unveiled before God (see 2 Corinthians 3:18). You will be honest with Him, yourself, and those with whom He asks you to be authentic. In addition, you will allow Him access to the most intimate part of your heart and trust Him with your emotions, desires, and hurts. If we do this, we will be ones that not only live by the Spirit, but walk by the Spirit as well (see Galatians 5:25). Not only will you shine brighter, but you will encourage others to do the same.

My earliest memory of my best friend was in elementary school. While I was in the third grade, our family moved to Pennsylvania where my parents bought the first of three businesses: The Big Star, a corner ice cream shop. Upon entering the fourth grade, I went to yet another new school. Three different schools in two years. I remember the first day, walking into my new school (due to a municipality zoning change), feeling left out, as most of the students had been together since kindergarten.

Everything seemed foreign to this little Jersey girl who was uprooted from a close lakeside community and a family-around-the-corner bond. But as soon as Miss Altemose uttered her first words, I felt at home. She, being my favorite elementary school teacher, introduced me to a girl with dark hair, a welcoming smile, and big heart. My fondest memory was spending time with my new best friend in her home and she at mine. It didn't matter what we did, from playing with Barbies to hitting the softball, as long as we were together.

Through the years, and many significant relationships later, what stands out to me is what I learned in the fourth grade: spending time together builds relationships.

Your personal friendships are no different than your most important friendship. The relationship above all others — your walk with God — is truly a girl's best friend. When your connection with God is healthy, it will create healthy relationships with people. When you place Him above all others, it will help you prioritize your friendships. Like diamonds, which get their brilliance from reflective light, He will be the Light you want to look into each day; and in return, you will reflect His love, joy, peace, patience, kindness, goodness, faithfulness, gentleness, and self-control in all other relationships.

TWEET:
When your connection with God is healthy, it will create healthy relationships with people.
#friendshipjourney

From the very beginning, God had a relationship with Adam and Eve that found them "walking in the garden in the cool of the day" (see Genesis 3:8). God created man for the enjoyment of a walking relationship that involved companionship, dialogue, intimacy, joint decision-making, mutual delight, and shared dominion. God longs to walk with you, which is why His arms of grace have been pulling you into a closer walk with Him.[1]

I came to enjoy and appreciate a book through a visit to a friend in South Carolina. We had just arrived to her southern-style home from the airport, and on her dining room table was this little black book with the title, *Secrets of the Secret Place* by Bob Sorge. It caught my eye. After asking her about it, I picked it up and discovered almost every page either highlighted or dog-eared. My first thought was, *I need to read this book!*

What I shortly found out from reading it was that the secret place is not the destination; it is only the catalyst that holds you together. It is designed by God to establish us in an intimate friendship with Him that is walked out through the course of our everyday lives.[2] The goal that we are after is an everyday walk, a 365-days-per-year friendship with our Lord, Savior, and friend.

The secret place with God is where we develop a walking relationship with Him.

Picture an iceberg. The secret place is what happens below the waterline. Most of us live our lives without giving much intentional thought to carving out the space necessary to shape lives of love, purpose, meaning, wisdom, and virtue.

Under the waterline of an iceberg is a large rock formation, which represents our time with Him. If you meet with God daily, that undergirding strength will increase and He will guide you in your everyday choices. It's what happens under the waterline that matters.

Enoch, the great-grandfather of Noah, was the first man in the Bible who walked with God.

> *Then Enoch walked with God three hundred years after he became the father of Methuselah, and he had other sons and daughters. So all the days of Enoch were three hundred and sixty-five years. Enoch walked with God; and he was not, for God took him.* — Genesis 5:22–24

Even though men began to call upon the name of the Lord in the early days (see Genesis 4:26), Enoch was the first man to uncover the true delight of walking with God. He found something even Adam didn't experience. He pressed into God until he learned how to commune with God through every facet of life. Enoch may have walked three hundred and sixty-five years with God, but I was soon feeling Him ask me to walk three hundred and sixty-five *days* with Him. Yes, every day! The more you meet with Him under the waterline through the length of your days with Him, this will increase your knowledge of His will in your life.

The more you continue to seek Him with all your heart, the more you will be enlightened with His truth.

The more you will be convicted by His desires.

The stronger you will become against adversity.

And the more sensitive you will be with others.

You will often hear me say, "I don't know what I am doing, I am just following God . . ."

For we are His workmanship, created in Christ Jesus for good works, which God prepared beforehand so that we would walk in them. — Ephesians 2:10

It is He that has prepared the way for you, for your ministry and for your life. All you need to do is walk in it.

What does walking with God look like?

By faith Enoch was taken up so that he did not see death, and he was not to be found because God took him up. For before his removal **he had been commended as having pleased God***. Now without faith it is impossible to please him, for the one who approaches God must believe that he exists and that he rewards those who seek him.* — Hebrews 11:5-6

All you need to do is please God with your everyday life, stay close to Him by meeting with Him, reading His Word, and following with great obedience what He asks you for this day. And let Him take care of the next day; He has already prepared it for you! Please don't close this book . . . stay with me.

Wow, as I reread that paragraph, my mind was flooded with early memories that didn't reflect a pretty picture. You see, the first five years of my walk with God, I didn't even open my Bible.

Oh yes, I was given a Bible at my conversion with my name engraved on it and then I thought, *what now?*

It didn't come with instructions and no one told me how to proceed.

As newlyweds, my husband and I found a good Bible-teaching church, but no discipleship. It was probably my own fault because I didn't even know to look for it.

I thought, *there must be more to this whole Christian thing.* So, then I was on a quest to find a Bible study . . .

And that is when the love of His Word first came to me.

I couldn't believe my eyes as I sat around a local woman's dining room table with ten other women of all ages and opened the book of Galatians. I thought, *this has been here the whole time, and I didn't know it?*

I'll be honest; initially, it wasn't easy to get into the Word of God.

It was flat-out work!

It was a discipline and a commitment.

But it eventually turned into delight and desire.

If you are reading the Bible and that is where you are, stick with it.

Never feel guilty for the time you spend in His Word.

Whoever we spend the most time with is who we will become!

It is the best thing you can do for yourself, your family, your church, and your workplace.

Being in His Word will become the starting place for your day.

We can trust in what His Word says to us about seeking Him:

> *... the LORD is with you when you are with Him. And if you seek Him, He will let you find Him; but if you forsake Him, He will forsake you.* —2 Chronicles 15:2b.

Yes, the Lord wants to have fellowship with us, but He will not force a relationship upon us. The choice is yours for the taking. It will need to be your daily choice to seek Him and allow His *guidance* in the quietness of your moments with Him.

Please flatter me by meditating on the word *guidance*.

What tends to stand out to you?

As I looked at guidance, I kept seeing *"dance"* at the end of the word.

I once read that doing God's will is a lot like dancing. When two people try to lead, nothing feels right.

The movement doesn't flow with the music, and everything is quite uncomfortable and jerky. When one person realizes that, and lets the other lead, both bodies begin to flow with the music. One gives gentle cues, perhaps with a nudge to the back or by pressing lightly in one direction or another. It's as if two become one body, moving together beautifully.

The dance takes surrender, willingness, and attentiveness from one person, and gentle guidance and skill from the other.

My eyes were drawn back to the word *guidance*.

When I saw "g" I thought of God, followed by "u" and "i": *God, "u" and "i" dance.*

"God, you, and I dance." [3]

As I lowered my head in obedience to His guidance, I became willing to put my life in His hands and allow Him to lead.

Won't you dance together with God, trusting Him to lead and to guide you through each season of your life?

Throughout Scripture we read countless times about those who walked with God and knew friendship with God from Enoch, Abraham (Genesis 6:9), Noah (Genesis 24:40), Job (Job 29:4), Zacharias (Luke 1:5-6), and on to Jesus. Through these men, in summary, we clearly see lessons such as: walking in the Spirit, not being conformed to this world, having perfect obedience and faithfulness in all things. This doesn't happen without being intentional about our secret place and time with Him.

Recently the story from Luke 24 has impacted my walk and friendship with God more than any other story. You may be familiar with it, but please let me recap it for you.

One day two of those who had been among Jesus were walking to a village in Emmaus discussing the day's finding. While they were walking, Jesus began to travel with them. But their eyes were prevented from recognizing Him. Jesus started to question them about the day's news and the two were astonished that their new traveling buddy was unaware of all that took place. They began to fill Jesus in of His own crucifixion and the empty tomb. As they approached their destination, they asked Him to remain with them and He did. They reclined at the table and dined with Jesus. As He broke bread with them, their eyes were opened and they recognized Him and then He vanished. They both recalled the burning sensation in their hearts as Jesus spoke with them and explained the Scriptures. They got up that very hour and returned to Jerusalem with the others and shared about their walk and the breaking of the bread with Jesus.

In this amazing story from Luke 24:13-35 what impressed me was that the two walked the same route back to Jerusalem but they were changed because they broke bread with Jesus. They must have had a little more bounce in their step. They had spent time with Him, the bread of Life (see John 6:48). Do you continue down the road a different person because you walk with Him? Or do you remain unchanged due to lack of luster?

When you follow Him with all your heart, soon you will join with the Lord and be one spirit with Him (see 1 Corinthians 6:17). Daily, you will be encouraged, challenged, and developed into what He wants you to be as you allow Him to teach you His ways, walk in His truth, and with your heart, give undivided attention to fear His name.

Teach me Your way, O Lord; I will walk in your truth; Unite my heart to fear Your name. —Psalm 86:11

When we walk with God, we enter the dimension where God unfolds the secrets of His kingdom (see Deuteronomy 29:29) and His will for your life.

The unfolding of His words gives light, and understanding to the simple (see Psalm 119:130).

What does your walk resemble in your daily life? Is it buffed, shiny and bright, or does it have a dull luster in need of a good shine?

A man's wisdom illumines him and causes his stern face to beam,
so don't be in such a hurry to leave Him (Ecclesiastes 8:1-3).

It may mean rising earlier in the morning.

Walking away from social media.

A step away from the lunch area at work or turning off the television.

It will be different for each of us, but what I can tell you is that it will be worth your time to follow His leading and trust Him with the outcome.

If you need a little giddy-up in your step, put your hand into His and let Him lead the dance, even if it is a slow dance. He will carry you until the beat takes hold and before you know it you are doing the Cha-Cha.

And through it all, He became this girl's best friend and He can become yours as well.

Chapter Two

My Forever Friend

A friend like you I would never want to replace because of the joys you bring in big and small ways, it makes you my friend forever and always. ~ Jessie Seneca

The night was long and lonely and thoughts were swirling with "what ifs." 'Twas the night before my left lung pneumonectomy.

The year was 2002.

Since 1992, I have fought a battle with Cushing's Syndrome, a life threatening disease. Five surgeries into it, I found myself facing the greatest of them all.

The removal of my left lung.

My husband, John, and I made the best out of our five-hour trip to the University of Virginia hospital with a wonderful autumn walk among the fallen leaves on the beautiful college campus, and a delicious meal the evening before the surgery. But as the night drew nigh, it became more difficult to think clearly.

To grasp all that lay ahead.

To envision life differently.

To accept the new normal.

To wonder if there would even be a tomorrow.

As we kissed goodnight and I turned over to sleep, facing a cold hotel wall, it was just me and God.

As I laid there trying to fall asleep, among many thoughts, I envisioned King Hezekiah.

In Isaiah 38:2, Hezekiah turned his face to the wall and prayed to God. God granted Hezekiah fifteen more years.

My prayer was to be able to raise my daughters and trust God with the outcome.

Life is not always a bowl of cherries. Sometimes we sit among the pits. But it is what we do while in the pits that matters. There is only one thing we can control in life and it is our attitude. I have heard it said, life is 10% what happens to me and 90% how I react to it. And so it is with you.

You are in charge of your attitude.

Honestly, so much of me wanted to curl up in a ball and not face any of it, but then there was so much of me that wanted to continue and live. What was I going to choose?

What are you going to choose?

It is your choice.

I call heaven and earth to witness against you today, that I have set before you life and death, the blessing and the curse. So choose life in order that you may live, you and your descendants, by loving the LORD your God, by obeying His voice, and by holding fast to Him; for this is your life and the length of your days, that you may live in the land which the LORD swore to your fathers, to Abraham, Isaac, and Jacob, to give them (Deuteronomy 30:19-20).

I choose life!

Oh, the thief tried to come steal, kill, and destroy, but He (Jesus) came that we may have life, and have *it* abundantly (see John 10:10).

I eventually fell asleep. Well, if you call it that. For a little while I drifted off, and then the tossing and turning began.

Off and on, shutting my eyes.

Sometime sleeping for minutes and sometimes a half hour.

Needless to say, it was a long night.

When I no longer could fall back to sleep in the dark, early hour of the morning, I arose and went into the bathroom as to not bother John. I found myself on the bathroom floor, praying, crying, and praying again . . . and then it happened to me.

Never before and never after, God spoke a poem into my heart for a dear friend.

I went and got the hotel pen and lined note paper and the words began to flow.

My Forever Friend

I often wish God blessed me long ago
   through the years of hopes and dreams
      but, He waited till this season of my life
      for our friendship, it seems

     Some friends come and some friends go
     and others we may never know
      but, friends like you, are a gift
       wrapped with a heavenly bow

    You're always there with a word
    to turn our eyes upon the Lord
     with keeping on your knees
    God is always pleased

    Friends may last a day
     and some friends through tomorrow
      then God gives us friends like you
       that are there through and through

    I enjoy our late night desires
    sipping tea by the fire
      bringing up new conversation
       and working through old frustrations

Your love and care
    are always there
        through the joys and sorrows
            you are continually there to uplift my tomorrow

Things will come and *Things* will go
    and *Things* will not matter, we know,
        but, in the end, it is the love we show
            with God's glorifying glow

A friend like you
    I would never want to replace
        because of the joys you bring in big and small ways
        it makes you my friend forever and always

Okay, I never said it was print quality, but it was from my heart back to God's ears.

Friendships: we all have them.

Some good and some not so good.

Some a joy and *some* that have been painful.

Before you continue reading, I want you to take a moment and think about the women and friendships in your life that have influenced you.

The good, the bad, and the ugly.

Think about how they have shaped you into who you have become.

Some of those thoughts are good and pleasant, and some may not be so good.

But, all of them have influenced you in one way or another. They have played into the woman you have become and are becoming.

Even when I think of some that haven't been so good, it reminds me that I may have learned the most from them. Learned what not to be and how not to act.

God uses all types and styles of friendships to make us more like Him!

In chapter one, we read the importance of our relationship with God. Yes, enjoying your relationship with Him will be the basis of all other friendships, but we also need God with skin.

In 1 Samuel 18:1-3 we read about one of the Bible's most famous friendships, David and Jonathan.

TWEET:
Enjoying your relationship with Him will be the basis of all other friendships.
#friendshipjourney

Now it came about when he had finished speaking to Saul, that the soul of Jonathan was knit to the soul of David, and Jonathan loved him as himself. Saul took him that day and did not let him return to his father's house. Then Jonathan made a covenant with David because he loved him as himself (1 Samuel 18:1-3).

Initially, David was liked by Saul, the king chosen by the people. Saul brought David in to help soothe him by playing his harp. But with David's rising popularity among the people, Saul became jealous of David after his victory over Goliath. Their relationship started to change due to the green-eyed monster of jealousy and resentment. But David was strengthened by the personal affection of Jonathan, Saul's oldest son and heir to the throne.

Jonathan knew God's favor was upon David, the king chosen by God.

Further on in 1 Samuel, we see David and Jonathan's friendship bond through empowerment and applause.

> *Now David became aware that Saul had come out to seek his life while David was in the wilderness of Ziph at Horesh. And Jonathan, Saul's son, arose and went to David at Horesh, and encouraged him in God. Thus he said to him, "Do not be afraid, because the hand of Saul my father will not find you, and you will be king over Israel and I will be next to you; and Saul my father knows that also." So the two of them made a covenant before the LORD; and David stayed at Horesh while Jonathan went to his house* (1 Samuel 23:15-18).

Much can happen in a wilderness experience.

We have all had them. An inhospitable event, situation, and yes, even friendship.

But what I would like to focus on in this chapter is a forever friendship.

A friendship that weathers the wilderness times, the moments of despair, the days of remorse and, equally as important, the successes of life.

In the wilderness of Horesh, we see Jonathan love his friend with deep care when he could have despised him. He encourages David to stay strong in his faith in God and not be afraid.

They both made a covenant, an agreement, before God and with each other to take care of one another.

Such warm sympathy, such glowing trustful words, you may well imagine, raised the spirits of David and gave him new courage to face the grave difficulties ahead of him.

That is the type of friend I desire to be.

Encourager.

Strengthener.

Sympathizer.

God fearer.

I know I will never get it all right, but it sure is worth the effort. Even if I try to be one of these to someone in the day before me, I will feel that I have accomplished great things.

Have you had the privilege to have this type of friendship?

A Jonathan and David relationship?

Soul sister friendship?

A forever friendship connection?

They can be few and far between.

As I look back over my life and reflect on the many friendships I have had, God has blessed me with a few Jonathan and David relationships in and out of the different seasons of my life. One in particular stands out to me.

She and her husband moved into our area after they were married and only remained for one year.

It was like a blink in time, but with much impact. It didn't seem fair that someone so special came into my life and just like that was gone. Why?

She from the south and me a northern girl my whole life, and we were both pregnant—me with my second and she with her first. After visiting our small church with few young couples, my pastor introduced us to each other and there was an instant bond that has sustained us through a move, child rearing, illnesses, challenges, and longgggggg phone calls. For that one, short-lived year, she and her husband soon became close-knit friends with our small circle of young married couples.

We may only visit each other every couple years, but it is a friendship that has a bond beyond comprehension. It is a friendship that picks up right where it left off and feels like you were never apart. You are comfortable with silence. You believe in that person and trust them with your friendship.

If I did not take the chance on friendship, I would have missed out on all that God wanted for me.

Some of you fear "putting yourself out there" because you have been hurt by someone you thought you could trust.

Loneliness happens when we don't take a chance and allow someone to get close to us. Sometimes you need to take that chance.

Many years ago, I met a woman in a mom's prayer group where our kids went to school together and, as we became better friends, she said to me, "At some point I may hurt you."

I responded, "I'll take that chance."

It wasn't too much, that a little pineapple ice cream and two spoons couldn't help.

I was so glad I took a chance on friendship. She has become my Forever Friend.

People have asked, how do you make friends?

Dale Carnegie said, "You can make more friends in two months by becoming interested in other people than you can in two years by trying to get other people interested in you." [4]

Being others-minded helps you watch for friends. Not expecting perfection in your friendships increases your chances, and allowing your friends to have other friends besides you also draws others to you.

One of the greatest things you can do for your friends is to let them off the hook.

Let them stand outside and watch at times.

Allow your friends to NOT be at the position of God.

The Garden of Gethsemane

Then Jesus came with them to a place called Gethsemane, and said to His disciples, "Sit here while I go over there and pray." And He took with Him Peter and the two sons of Zebedee (James and John), and began to be grieved and distressed. Then He said to them, My soul is deeply grieved,

*to the point of death; remain here and keep watch with Me."
And He went a little beyond them, and fell on His face and
prayed, saying, "My Father, if it is possible, let this cup
pass from Me; yet not as I will, but as You will." And He
came to the disciples and found them sleeping, and said to
Peter, "So, you men could not keep watch with Me for one
hour? Keep watching and praying that you may not enter
into temptation; the spirit is willing, but the flesh is weak"*
(Matthew 26:36-41).

Yes, we have to at times—as Jesus went a little beyond with
His Father and asked His friends to stay behind to pray—that is
what we have to allow for our friends.

We have to allow them to be on the outside, watching while
we do business with God.

Oh, yes, by all means ask them to be praying with you and
for you. But then there is a time to release them and you have
your private meeting with your Father.

In that secret place with Him, that little beyond abode, He
will disclose Himself to you and you will experience the Master's
touch, which will allow you to move out with confidence and
security.

Many times, our expectations are too high for our friends to
keep up with.

We think they should know when we wake up on the wrong
side of the bed.

They should know we are worn out from trying to be everything to everyone.

And wonder, *why have they not called me?*

Why have they not written me?

Why have they not "liked" my Facebook post?

Guess what? They have "stuff" happening, too.

But more importantly, remember our friends are NOT to be in the position of God.

Allow them some slack; they are mere humans.

It is just as when I rolled over in my bed the night before my surgery. As great as the touch of my husband was, when I turned over it was just me and God.

It is just you and God, the best friend a girl can have.

Are you allowing Him His rightly seat?

Chapter Three

Friend or Foe

In the end, we will remember not the words of our enemies
but the silence of our friends ~ Martin Luther King, Jr.

In chapter two, I asked you to take a moment and think about the women and friendships in your life that have influenced you.

The good, the bad, and the ugly.

How you think about yourself and how they have shaped you into who you have become.

Some of those thoughts are good and pleasant and some may not be so good.

You know the person.

The one who hurt you.

The one who betrayed you.

The one who walked with you and, for one reason or the other, turned away from you.

The one who you thought would be your forever friend, but slowly substituted others for you and eventually you stopped hearing from her.

Most often you are not betrayed by an enemy but a companion.

Even though there may be hints of positive thought, they are clouded over with hurtful memories. I want to encourage you. We all have these relationships. They are not fun and maybe you even wish they never happened. I know. I lived a couple myself.

But when looking back on them, they may have been the best thing for me.

At the time, it seemed almost debilitating and a cause to stop ministry, work, or possibly living.

As I already mentioned, they have influenced me in one way or another.

They have played into the woman I have become and the ministry God ordained.

I recall a time when God opened a door to something that I thought would be the most amazing experience. And yes, it started out that way. But soon after, it slowly started to spiral out of control to the point that I stepped away one week out from the event along with a few others.

Friendships started to turn south and leadership styles looked very different.

I vividly remember coming home from the meeting after I resigned and walked into a dark home. My husband had already been tucked into bed for many hours.

Honestly, I didn't have the heart to wake him, as he had pleaded with me six months prior to step away. These were his exact words, " You will pull out one week before the event."

I thought, *what?*

No way, I am doing this for God and not for man. I can do this for the betterment of our community and our local women. So I marched on . . .

That heartbreaking night when I resigned, I took my spot on the family room couch and vowed to never do ministry again. Never, I say.

The long night soon came to an end with the breaking of dawn.

The days to follow were difficult, but the presence of God and a few companions helped me to continue ahead and hold my head above water.

The event came and went, and, if you are wondering, I did attend the event along with 4,800 other women. It was a success and our community was forever changed by His spoken Word. The fervent relationship that started out strong ended after eighteen months, never to be recaptured, but became a watermark on my heart that rippled through my mind's eye for over a decade.

As quickly as the event ended, so did that relationship. One to never be touched again.

But the effects lasted much beyond the conference.

A friendship for a season.

A relationship for a reason.

What man meant for harm, God meant for good.

Misery became ministry.

Learned lessons went before me toward God's call on my life. Lessons of obedience, trust, and faith.

But you say, "I never suspected it."

Or maybe like me, you saw it slowly declining, but wanted to try and salvage it.

Although, in the end it didn't work out as planned.

There was a man in the Old Testament, King David, who found himself questioning a friendship that went awry. A friendship that started out well, but ended poorly.

A man who, like you and me, was bewildered at a turn of events.

Look at David's response.

For it is not an enemy who reproaches me, then I could bear it; nor is it one who hates me who has exalted himself against me, then I could hide myself from him. But it is you, a man my equal, My companion and my familiar friend; We who had sweet fellowship together, walked in the house of God in the throng . . . As for me, I shall call upon God . . . His speech was smoother than butter, but his heart was war; His words were softer than oil, yet they were drawn swords. Cast your burden upon the Lord and He will sustain you;

He will never allow the righteous to be shaken. So, who will you trust to sustain you? (Psalm 55:12-16, 21-22).

Who will you and I allow to carry us when the hurt arises?

Will you follow David's example and call upon God? It's truly the only way to walk through the disappointment, the defeat, the frustration, and come out victorious.

Even Jesus, Himself, at the Last Supper experienced betrayal by a friend.

> *As they were reclining at the table and eating, Jesus said, "Truly I say to you that one of you will betray Me — one who is eating with me . . . it is one of the twelve, one who dips with Me in the bowl"* (Mark 14:18, 20).

This was a betrayal that cost Him His life, but He knew His purpose was to serve, and to give His life as a ransom for many (see Mark 10:45).

Jesus not only experienced betrayal by Judas, who you and I may characterize as a foe, but also experienced denial from His dear friend, Peter, when he denied Him three times before the rooster crowed.

Though Jesus' internal struggle with Judas' betrayal is not recorded in Scripture, we can assume that it was difficult for Him. I am sure Jesus experienced a flood of emotions to both men as they were intricately a part of His life and ministry.

Judas and Peter both had sorrow over what they had done. But there was a big difference in the nature of their sorrow: Judas had a sorrow that led only to regret (see Matthew 27:3) and eventual despair. Peter had a sorrow that went beyond regret— all the way to a transformed life—a life changed for an eternal purpose and call.

Just as both David and Peter responded, so should our first response be to cry out to Jesus who loves us, pursues us, and intimately understands the reality of betrayal.

I still find myself asking, "Friend or Foe?" over my lost friendship and broken trust.

In reality, some may think a foe, but when looking back, through the lens of my difficult situation, it taught me much and allowed me to learn valuable lessons that I would have not learned if I didn't walk this road of hardship. What seemed like a foe became a friend in time. A friend to life experiences, personal evaluation, and God-sized dreams.

Maybe you are reading this and you have experienced something similar. You are in the throes of a sour relationship or there is that *someone* who just won't let you unwrap the grave cloths and let you go (see John 11:44). It is time to throw off the old and put on the new.

> Do not call to mind the former things, or ponder things of the past. "Behold, I will do something new, now it will spring forth; will you not be aware of it? I will even make a roadway in the wilderness, rivers in the desert" (Isaiah 43:18-19).

There is light at the end of the tunnel. There is hope for the hurts. I know this is a cliché saying, *time will heal the hurts,* but you will need to allow God access to your heart, mind, and soul; and over time, He will fade the memory and soften the blow if we allow Him full access.

You ask, how do you move forward from a *foe* relationship?

While reading Hebrews 12:1-2, I was encouraged to throw off those things that hinder me.

Therefore, since we have so great a cloud of witnesses surrounding us, let us also lay aside every encumbrance and the sin which so easily entangles us, and let us run with endurance the race that is set before us, fixing our eyes on Jesus, the author and perfecter of faith, who for the joy set before Him endured the cross, despising the shame, and has sat down at the right hand of the throne of God (Hebrews 12:1-2).

Yes, first, throw off every encumbrance.

In the Greek, *encumbrance (ogkos)* [5] means whatever is prominent, protuberance, bulk, mass; hence a burden or weight. An encumbrance can be a situation or person. This is not sin but baggage.

Baggage that stops you from moving forward. It's not always bad things, but it keeps you from doing what God wants you to do.

Yes, there might be some people that hold you back, but it can also be yourself that you find to be the foe. Ouch!

You may be holding onto things that don't characterize you any longer. Things God is asking you to walk away from, burdens you have carried too long, regrets and resentments that weigh you down. It might just be you who is holding onto the grave cloths.

Secondly, He wants us to lay aside the sins that entangle us. The sin of unbelief, the sin of not obeying what God asks of you. Are you becoming attached to anything that continues to hurt God? Turn away.

> *The eye is the lamp of the body; so then if your eye is clear, your whole body will be full of light. But if your eye is bad, your whole body will be full of darkness. If then the light that is in you is darkness, how great is the darkness! "No one can serve two masters; for either he will hate the one and love the other, or he will be devoted to one and despise the other. You cannot serve God and wealth"* (Matthew 6:22-24).

God wants you to run your race lean and mean.

This will take daily editing on your part. A daily time with a girl's best friend, our Lord.

This race will take endurance.

Yes, it is hard. In the Greek, *race (agone)* [6] from Hebrews 12:1, means agony, effort—conflict, contention, fight, race.

Life is not a walk in the park at times . . . sometimes it is just plain hard. Running a race is exhausting and challenging. But if you want to stand on the winner's stand and receive the reward, you have to plow through agony, weariness, and tiresome times with power, love, and discipline to guard the treasure within and fulfill the ministry before you.

Thirdly, but the most important, *Fix your eyes on Jesus* (see Hebrews 12:2).

When the road seems long and the fight is hard, Jesus can lighten the load.

> *Have you not heard? The Everlasting God, the LORD, the Creator of the ends of the earth does not become weary or tired. His understanding is inscrutable. He gives strength to the weary, and to him who lacks might He increases power . . . Yet those who wait for the LORD will gain new strength; they will mount up with wings like eagles. They will run and not get tired, they will walk and not become weary* (Isaiah 40:28-31).

He has already run it and He has prepared it for you. Won't you trust Him with the outcome?

> *For you are His workmanship, created in Christ Jesus for good works, which God prepared beforehand so that we would walk in them* (Ephesians 2:10).

As I spoke of this chapter to a dear friend, she questioned, "Is it okay to grieve the loss of a relationship? It seems, in order to grow, I need to grieve."

Yes, that is a natural part of loss. Loss of a marriage, loss to death, or loss of a friendship; they all take the grieving process of denial, anger, bargaining, depression, and finally acceptance.

As I have grieved the loss of relationships, I've wondered, *How, why, and where did it all go wrong?*

Was it my fault? What could I have done differently in order for the outcome to look different?

This can be a humbling process, but humility says,

"Lord, I am empty without Your fullness; I am broken without Your wholeness; I am helpless without Your strength; I am clueless without Your wisdom. Apart from You I am nothing. I need You! I need You so desperately that I am pouring myself out to You here in the secret place." [7]

When we meet with the Lord like this, He reveals things to us that only He is able to show us through deep provoking conversation known as prayer.

Grief is a natural process, but hopefully after a time of reflection—and, if needed, counseling—you are able to grapple with the emotions, feelings, and differences that present themselves and grow from them.

You may never like the reality of the loss, but eventually you will need to accept it. You learn to live with it. It is the new normal with which you must learn to live. And you are able to take all that you learned into your next relationship, business endeavor, or ministry.

Yes, give grief its time but don't get stuck in the wallowing. Invest in new relationships and take the first step, move out, change, grow, and evolve into the person you are becoming.

Through all of life's experiences and relationships you encounter, hopefully it will give you a desire to grow from them and want to display outwardly what is happening inwardly, because when you allow God to transform your thinking through what you believe about Him, you will want to make a difference in someone else's life.

As you are driven deep into the Word of God due to a situation or personality conflict, you will experience God as your healer, provider, deliverer, sustainer, and friend. It will allow you to accept a situation, give you strength to approach another, or walk away from a hurtful relationship.

It may even allow you to see yourself for who you are.

Yikes, that is a tough one.

Has this ever happened to you? You enter your prayer time with God about a particular situation and in the middle of your prayer, the tables are turned upside down and you find yourself seeing it from the other person's position?

God reveals some ugliness in your own heart that needs cleansing and you find yourself in need of forgiveness.

It is in that moment with God that you need to make a decision: are you going to humble yourself before Him and allow Him to transform your thinking, attitude, and response?

Now, listen to me. This is a very intimate moment with God. It may just be between you and Him and no one needs to know the intricacy of your time, but you will come out different than when you entered. You will evolve from your time with Him more sensitive, wiser, and more prudent.

TWEET: Words may never need to be exchanged, but your actions will speak clearly for others to see. #friendshipjourney

Words may never need to be exchanged, but your actions will speak clearly for others to see.

Don't misunderstand. There are times words are needed and necessary, but not always.

There are times it is just you and God, and other times will call for you to be authentic with all, transparent with most, and intimate with some.[8]

Guard your heart and mouth and tread lightly when sharing your deepest thoughts, desires, and dreams.

In the next chapter, we will learn more about what to do when some of our friendships come to an end.

Chapter Four

Now What? Move On!

Love is the only force capable of transforming an enemy into friend. ~ Martin Luther King, Jr.

Things happen.

Things happen to the best of us.

Sometimes they are not even intentional, but they happen.

What do we do with those emotions, those hurts, and those differences?

In the last chapter, we established that there are friendships that come to an abrupt end.

When that happens, *Now What?*

We have to shake off the dust and move on.

Move on, learning from the good and the not-so-good.

Allowing God to sanctify you and use you to be instruments for His special purposes, made holy, useful to the Master and prepared to do any good work (see 2 Timothy 2:21).

I love how Scripture includes inspiring acts of heroism but at the same time doesn't cover up the messiness of real life.

Saul of Tarsus had been such a vicious persecutor of Christians that, even after his conversion, the brethren were still afraid of him. When Paul eventually returned to Jerusalem following his conversion to Christ, Barnabas had to persuade the disciples to let Paul fellowship with them (see Acts 9:26). As a result of this intercession, a wonderful friendship between Paul and Barnabas was formed. It is, therefore, rather sad to note that they eventually had a "falling out" of sorts.

On their first missionary journey together, John Mark, the cousin of Barnabas (see Colossians 4:10), accompanied them. Along the way, however, John Mark decided to return to his home in Jerusalem (see Acts 13:13). The reason for his departure is not mentioned.

Later on, when a second mission was planned, Barnabas proposed taking John Mark along, but Paul resisted the idea.

Acts 15:36-41 indicates that a "sharp disagreement" developed between them. They could not reach an agreement, and so they separated.

TWEET:
One failure doesn't mean unfruitfulness. #friendshipjourney

As far as the sacred record indicates, these two remarkable men never saw one another again. [9]

This is another instance of Barnabas' patience with the failures of others. He was the son of encouragement (see Acts 4:36). He wanted to give John Mark another chance. Every time I think about the relationship with Barnabas and John Mark, I am so thankful for second chances.

Thankful that this one failure by John Mark did not stop him from continued use.

Barnabas saw something in him that still needed tending to. Remember, Barnabas' name means *encouragement*. He was living up to that name.

I once heard it said that Paul had his eye on the goal, while Barnabas had his eye on the man.

Their disagreement was so deep that it couldn't be resolved, and these veterans whose friendship went back at least 15 years, and who owed each other so much, parted company. Neither would yield.

However, Paul would later affectionately mention Barnabas as being worthy of monetary support in his work of proclaiming the gospel (see 1 Corinthians 9:6).

And later in time, Mark became useful again to Paul as revealed in the apostle's concluding epistle. "Get Mark and bring him with you, for he is useful to me for ministering" (see 2 Timothy 4:11). And in Colossians 4:10, one observes that the once-rejected young worker was commended, and the Colossian saints were asked to be receptive to him.

It pains our heart to see brothers and sisters divided. But the fact remains, good and godly believers (even church leaders!)

may sharply disagree and, as a result, divide into separate spheres of ministry.

This wasn't a disagreement over one of the fundamentals of the faith, but one of personality.

Who was right?

We may never know this side of eternity, but what we do know is that they reached more people for Christ separate than together.

This is clearly a case of *agree to disagree.*

Now what?

Move on.

Take, for instance, another conflict, this time between two women in the church at Philippi: Eudia and Syntyche. We really don't know much about them other than the fact that they were not in agreement with one another. It must have been pretty ugly and public for the apostle Paul to send out word to one of the elders there to "help these women . . . to come together in unity" (see Philippians 4:2-3).

If you've been in church for any length of time, participated in a Women's Ministry — or possibly your own family, for that matter — you've probably witnessed a "Eudia" or a "Syntyche" in action.

You know what I mean: even though they are well-meaning ladies and work for the gospel, their cutting remarks, the glares across the room, the rolling of eyes, the cold dispositions, and the argumentative spirits are more than one can stand.

Sometimes it's not so obvious, but when there's a noticeable division, it puts the entire body out of whack.

It creates a division within the body of believers.

For even as the body is one and yet has many members, and all the members of the body, though they are many, are one body, so also is Christ . . . But God has so composed the body, giving more abundant honor to that member which lacked, so that there may be no division in the body, but that the members may have the same care for one another (1 Corinthians 12:12, 24-25).

Ironic, isn't it, that the appeal to the Philippian church comes straight from Paul, the man with the sharp disagreement?

I am not implying anything, only to say that maybe Paul learned a practical lesson from a personal incident.

Paul's appeal for someone to serve as a peacemaker is an appeal to us, as well.

Sometimes, we have to step out of our comfort zone to keep peace with another sister.

I know this can be hard.

I have been on the receiving end as well as the giving side.

It calls for humility, vulnerability, and can be downright scary.

But I will say this: if it is what God is calling you to do, you must do it.

If you don't follow through with what He is asking you to do, it will fester and a root of bitterness will blossom into full-blown resentment.

This I know, freedom comes with obedience.

I know from the giving side, if I didn't share what was in my heart with the other person, knowing it was what God wanted me to do, it would have felt like a slow death until I approached them. A heaviness I could not shake.

It had been many years since I needed to practice relationship resolutions, and wouldn't you know it, in the midst of writing this book two different situations arose within one month that needed recovering.

Neither one was catastrophic, but they still needed to be addressed.

As I stepped back and looked at both situations, it could have been a ploy by the evil one to distract me or stop me from writing on this important topic of friendship.

Swirling around in my head, *who am I, anyway, to take this on?*

But the Lord had a different outcome in mind. Each situation very different from the other, but both ended with a strengthened relationship.

One morning during my devotions around the time these encounters happened, my reading for that day took me to 1 Peter 4:8-9: *Above all, keep fervent in your love for one another, because love covers a multitude of sins. Be hospitable to one another without complaint.*

Isn't that just like God to give you just what you need at that very moment and encourage you with His Word?

I am convinced as you and I continue to draw near to God, He draws near to us (see James 4:8) and provides for us as we need it.

I have had both situations in my life.

Some I wished would have ended differently than they did.

And others that were strengthened.

What I do know is that both were approached with resolution in mind.

Both had the same end goal in mind, but came out differently.

You are only accountable for your own actions and attempts.

If the other party does not receive it from you and you have done all you can, you must dust off your feet and walk upright.

You must continue, despite disagreements and division.

You must persevere, forgetting what lies behind and reaching forward to what lies ahead (see Philippians 3:13) while still striving to live out 1 Corinthians 13:4-7 (MSG):

> *So, no matter what I say, what I believe, and what I do, I'm bankrupt without love.*
> *Love never gives up.*
> *Love cares more for others than for self.*
> *Love doesn't want what it doesn't have.*
> *Love doesn't strut,*

Doesn't have a swelled head,
Doesn't force itself on others,
Isn't always "me first." Doesn't fly off the handle,
Doesn't keep score of the sins of others,
Doesn't revel when others grovel,
Takes pleasure in the flowering of truth,
Puts up with anything,
Trusts God always,
Always looks for the best,
Never looks back,
But keeps going to the end.

These verses are the most eloquent and profound words ever written on the subject of love and they are ones to daily practice.

I want to end this chapter with a sweet story that I just observed last week at the end of our church service.

While talking with a small group of friends, a friend's daughter was standing with us.

As we stood around conversing, out of the corner of my eye, I saw another young girl, no older than ten or eleven, waiting in the wings, just looking for the right time to approach our circle.

One of the ladies with us asked the young girl, "Did you want to talk to one of us?" The young girl, without hesitation, walked to my friend's daughter and proceeded to share her heart.

She said, "Do you remember me? We were at Vacation Bible School together last summer."

My friend's daughter replied, "No," looking baffled as to what she was going to say next.

The young girl continued, "I treated you poorly and was not nice to you. It has been bothering me for a while and I wanted to come to you and say, I am sorry for how I treated you."

My friend's daughter graciously accepted her unnecessary apology.

Maybe unnecessary to one, but very necessary to another.

The young girl who apologized was carrying that baggage around for over a year.

What a sweet spirit she had.

You can bet she walked away relieved and with a new lease on life.

That moment was not just for my friend's daughter, but for the grown-up girls looking on.

Chapter Five

Sistering

Sistering is two women coming together to share their hearts and lives and when they depart from their time together each one believes they were the one that got the greatest blessing.
~ Linda Williams

What comes to your mind as you read the title of this chapter?

Sistering.

Sisterhood, caring friends, love?

Exactly!

Sisterhood, done right, can be one of the best parts of our lives as women. We need these relationships. We want these relationships. We long for these relationships.

The suffix *-ing,* defined from Merriam-Webster's dictionary, denotes a verbal action relating to an occupation or skill.[10]

So sister*ing* would mean a woman or girl in relation to other daughters and sons of her parents or a close female friend or associate acting out her role.

Then, sister*ing* is an action verb.

Through the years of being involved with Women's Ministry and sharing at events, sisterhood and friendship is one of the hot topics women question me about. It is part of our DNA to cultivate lasting relationships with other women. Even though, at times, we experience hurtful situations, we still desire them because we are meant to build into each other's lives. We are meant for relationships, not isolation.

TWEET:
Sisterhood, done right, can be one of the best parts of our lives as women. #friendshipjourney

You will never achieve your maximum spiritual potential without the help of those key relationships God places around you. Yet, in order to benefit from these friendships, you must open your heart and take the risk of being a friend and of sistering.

Effective body life begins with each individual being rightly related to God in an intimate love relationship. It continues as all the members are rightly related to Jesus Christ as the Head of the church. Right relationships with God are far more important than buildings, budgets, programs, methods, church personnel, size, or anything else.[11]

Allowing God to work through you will make the body more complete.

We are sisters for a journey.

I do not have a blood sister, and I guess there is a part of me that always secretly desired a sister. I watch other sisters care for one another, trade clothes, and enjoy each other's families as though they were their own. They seem to always have someone to pick up the phone and talk with one another, have lunch together, and share their deepest cares, struggles, and victories. I know there are some sisters that are not this fortunate, but the portrayal seems surreal.

I just came home from returning a borrowed item from my neighbor and didn't keep it a secret that I wanted in on their family sisterhood. She shared with me what she was doing the following month. She and her two sisters made a pact while growing up to celebrate their fiftieth birthdays by going away to an island. The two that are celebrating the sister's birthday pay for the trip, and they were heading to Jamaica. What a great idea: undivided attention, deep conversation, and quality time spent with each other.

Jealous? Me too!

Oh wait, I do have these relationships . . . and so do you! Okay, maybe not a paid vacation, but I have plenty of sisters in the Lord that do exactly these things: undivided attention, deep conversation, and quality time spent with each other.

My "sister friends" reach out, encourage, care, walk alongside through difficulties, and sometimes they even share their clothes.

In our first year of marriage, God blessed John and me with friendship with the only other young couple in our church. It was an instant friendship between both parties. We seemed to spend endless hours with each other and talk into the wee hours of the morning, sharing dreams and expectations. We became the closest thing to blood sisters that we were allowed. Even through a move many states away, there is plenty of *sistering* still happening. This year, we celebrate thirty years of friendship, family weddings, and a bond that cannot be broken.

I think the most I have learned about friendships is from watching others do it so well and wanting to embody their example.

In chapter two, I mentioned how I have fought the fight of Cushing's Syndrome. Through the past twenty-plus years, I have seen my friends and family share the love of Jesus and use their gifts to come alongside me and my family in many ways.

> *Two people are better off than one, for they can help each other succeed. If one person falls, the other can reach out and help. But someone who falls alone is in real trouble. Likewise, two people lying close together can keep each other warm. But how can one be warm alone? A person standing alone can be attacked and defeated, but two can stand back-to-back and conquer. Three are even better, for a triple-braided cord is not easily broken* (Ecclesiastes 4:9-12, NLT).

You can have the full body of armor on and stand firm. With the belt of truth buckled around your waist.

The breastplate of righteousness in place.

Your feet fitted with the readiness that comes from the gospel of peace.

You can take up the shield of faith, with which you can extinguish all the flaming arrows of the evil one.

Put on the helmet of salvation.

Have the sword of the Spirit, which is the Word of God.

But still have your backside uncovered (see Ephesians 6:10-17).

As you look at Ecclesiastes 4:9-12, you will see when two believers come together with the full armor of God on and standing back-to-back they can conquer whatever is in front of them.

They will be completely covered on all sides, even their backs.

But the most important piece of the armor is prayer.

With all prayer and supplication pray at all times in the Spirit (see Ephesians 6:18).

If you have a faithful praying sister upholding you, you are a fortunate and a blessed girl. Prayer is the catalyst of a strong friendship. So, you must allow others to join you.

Uphold you.

We are sisters for a journey.

I have been on the receiving end of sisters coming around me for prayer and recall the sense of peace and tranquility that surrounded those moments. But I vividly remember visiting a friend while she was recovering from surgery, listening to all she learned with God in the quietness of her recliner. In that moment, I felt God nudge me to pray with her. The battle in my mind began, Will she receive and accept it?

God, are you sure?

I knew I needed to pray for her out of pure obedience to God. So, I knelt at her feet with my hands on her lap and began to pray over her.

It was exactly what God ordained.

For a moment, time seemed to stop with His presence so vivid.

Days later, with gained strength she shared with me the meaning of our time together.

Without friends, you will not only fall, but you will become extremely lonely.

Two are good because you have a friend that can assist, but three are even better, for a triple-braided cord is not easily broken.

Sistering is a little like riding a triplet, a three-seater tandem bike. You have the captain—the person who sits on the front seat, who guides and directs—while the stoker, the person on the back seat assists in the ride. The stoker really has to trust the person captaining the bike, and the captain has to rely on a stoker who maintains a steady position and is responsive to the choices the captain makes. It is a team approach.

Tandem riding develops communication skills, builds trust, and cultivates respect for each other's strengths.

I say a triplet tandem bike because, just as Ecclesiastes 4:12 tells us three are even better, so it is, as we ride through life. When you have Jesus Christ as a partner with two believing friends, you form an even stronger bond.

When Jesus is in the center of your relationship, He directs the ride and leads you in the direction that is best.

We certainly need to have our closest friends and family on the journey with us.

Therefore I urge you, brethren, by the mercies of God, to present your bodies a living and holy sacrifice, acceptable to God, which is your spiritual service of worship (Romans 12:1).

God wants us to be a *living* sacrifice — to let Him have all our strengths that have been saved and sanctified through Jesus. This is what is accepting to Him.

This is not a sacrifice that takes your lives away from you, but one that requires we keep on living.

As a child of God, you and I have the opportunity to offer our bodies as a living sacrifice to bring glory to Jesus. Instead of using my body in acts of triviality, I can, if I choose to, be a part of God's eternal plan and have His power working through me (see Colossians. 1:29).

Then my hands, eyes, feet, and tongue — and all my other body parts — will be living sacrifices to God. And this leads to holiness and purpose in my life. Presenting your body as a living sacrifice becomes a privilege for the equipping of the saints and building up the body.[12]

If we start our day before God with the mentality of giving Him ourselves—not just one part, but all functioning parts of ourselves—we will go through the rest of our day more God-conscious.

More watchful of serving Him in small and big ways.

It is one of the best ways to prepare yourself for the day ahead, because it reminds you that you are not your own, you are bought with a price. And therefore, your body—every part of it—should be a living sacrifice all day long, every day.

You and I are servants of God, and every part of your body should be under His control.

Sometimes we don't even realize we are in the middle of a sacrifice until after the effects are behind us.

Recently, while dining with a friend, I shared a deep concern of mine. As we lingered over dinner and deep conversation, she was able to give me wise counsel that encouraged me to take the step I needed to take.

The next day, I realized all that God allowed to occur to make that conversation happen.

The obedience to send a spur of the moment text to my friend, both husbands out of town, reservations available on a Friday night at a busy restaurant, a corner table away from the crowd and a *yes* from my friend to join me.

This was a triplet tandem ride. One guiding, one following, and the Holy Spirit leading.

Because I know my friend starts her day out before the Lord, she was sensitive to the leading of the Holy Spirit in that very precious moment.

Other times, we consciously make the decision to obey and lay our lives on the altar for another.

Let me share about one dear friend and how God called her to journey with us.

She sacrificed herself and her own daily life for mine.

She brought everything she was involved with to a screeching halt to take care of our two girls (a toddler and an infant) four days a week, so John would not have to put them into daycare during the onset of my disease and four-month hospital stay.

She cared for my girls as if they were her very own, along with her elementary-age boys. Months later, after I recovered, I asked her why and how she did it. She responded, "I was doing it unto God and the Holy Spirit gave me the strength I needed every day." The effect of this sacrificial act of kindness went far beyond our immediate family. It also touched the lives of all who knew her and is still touching those that read about her self-sacrificing love for a friend.

She was the greatest example of friendship to me.

Not only was my life touched by and through her, but our girls' lives were, too. Their relationship with her went from caregiver to friend; through years of grade school lunch dates, high school tears, cards of encouragement, and hours of conversation. They were touched by sistering.

So much so that when our youngest daughter, Sarah, got married, she came to me and asked, "Would it be okay for 'Big' Sarah and her husband to walk down the aisle before the grandparents?"

You see how the effects of one person's obedience and sacrifice can reach more than just yourself?

Not only was this moment one to be cherished by our family, but also by those who knew her and that her sacrifices were moved by her deep dedication to follow God with her daily life.

> *Since we have gifts that differ according to the grace given to us, each of us is to exercise them accordingly . . .* (Romans 12:6a).

We each have been given a gift, some of us multiple gifts; natural abilities and Spiritual gifts. All that we are given is to edify and encourage the body. These gifts are not for us alone, but for one another. Paul encouraged Timothy *to kindle afresh* (NASB), *to fan into flame* (NIV) *the gift of God which was in him* (see 1 Timothy 2:6).

Whether kindling afresh or fanning into flame, they both denote actively using your gift(s) to serve the Lord.

For so long, I thought I would find this kindling from another person. But what I realized is that it can only come from drawing close to our Father. Coming before an audience of One is enough to carry you through anything He is calling you to do, from helping a friend, visiting a shut-in, stepping out in faith, taking a risk, confronting a coworker, or delving into the realm of the unknown.

Gloria McDonald, in her book, *High Call, High Privilege,* says, "Untended fires soon die and become just a pile of ashes."[13]

Not only do we need to tend to the inner fire, but also fan into flame the gifts He has given us. If not, they will become worthless and void of effectiveness.

We need to remember that, whether it is a natural ability or a spiritual gift, everything that we have is a gift of God's grace (see Ephesians 4:7). Thus, none of us can boast in our gifts.

> *Every good thing given and every perfect gift is from above, coming down from the Father of lights, with whom there is no variation or shifting shadow* (James 1:17).

All He asks us to do is use them for His glory.

You would be nothing without Him!

You may be thinking, *My gift is not as good as the giftedness in my friend.* Or, *I wish I had so-and-so's gift.* That is not for us to determine.

He calls you and me to stay in our lanes.

The phrase, *stay in your lane,* makes me laugh every time.

I am just as guilty as you might be of crossing lanes at times.

My family always tells me when I go out to speak, "Mom, stay in your lane."

You see, I am not that funny, and when I try to be, I get taken off focus. I move out of my lane.

I come home with stories—funny stories, may I add.

My assistant will text my girls: *your mama went out of her lane tonight.*

All joking aside . . .

God wants you and me to keep our eyes on the giver of the gift and work hard to use the gift bestowed upon us.

Therefore my beloved sister, be steadfast, immovable, always abounding in the work of the Lord, knowing that your toil is not in vain in the Lord (1 Corinthians 15:58).

Your sistering is for a higher call. A calling beyond yourself. May you not lose heart while doing good.

Chapter Six

Be a Friend to Have a Friend

Even the most independent and certainly the most isolated among us need community. Never fail to express the simple but powerful message: I am thinking of you. ~ Dawn Camp

As I sit writing this book, my furry, four-legged friends are not far away. Actually, they both lie at my feet and sometimes when they are ready for me to be done writing, Murphy jumps up on the back of my chair and wraps himself around me.

Now, these dogs are not small.

They are two golden-doodles weighing close to seventy pounds each.

So picture that, a seventy-pound ball of fur as a lap dog.

It is said, dogs are a (wo)man's best friend.

Most of you who have a dog will agree.

We certainly can learn from our dogs how to be friends.

They have your back; they mimic your emotions, listen to your complaints, and motivate you. And, they eventually start looking like you. They won't leave you hanging or let you eat alone, and they act as mini-dishwashers.

We love our dogs. They are a big part of our family.

Don't tell the rest of my family, but I am pretty sure I am our dogs' favorite. Ha!

When our girls went off to college, I think they missed the dogs more than they missed us. Based on the tone of your voice and your body language, your dog will do its darnedest to emulate your current state of mind. When you are sad, they'll look at you with big doe eyes. When you're angry, the fur will rise on their backs and they'll start barking and growling at lifeless objects. Whereas humans might not respond to your emotional upswings and downswings in a way that you'd prefer, dogs will always be there whether you're happy, depressed, or anywhere in between.

They motivate you to exercise.

There aren't many days we don't go for our daily walk — yes, for my sanity, but mostly for them to release some much-needed energy.

I remember when our daughter, Sarah, was a little girl, she would always say she was going to marry Buster (our late beagle). I think over the years our dogs heard more secrets from our girls than they cared to know. But they were vaulted forever.

Hmmmm . . . So, do you think we can learn a little something from our canines on how to be a friend?

I believe part of the reason my dogs love me so much is because I care for them, I feed them, I hug and love on them,

I walk them, and, yes, even talk to them. And I absolutely put their needs before mine on that wintry, cold, twenty-degree day when I take them for their daily walk, looking like the Michelin lady.

Do you and I go out of our way for our friends like this?

Or are we too busy for relationships?

I know I quoted Dale Carnegie in another chapter, but it can be heard over and over again. "You can make more friends in two months by becoming interested in other people than you can in two years by trying to get other people interested in you."[14]

How can you move from being isolated to developing close friendships?

A man who has friends must himself be friendly (Proverbs 18:24a, NKJV).

You can't wait for a friend to reach out to you.

Take the first step and be willing to break the stalemate.

British preacher Charles Spurgeon put it this way: "Any man can selfishly desire to have a Jonathan; but he is on the right track who desires to find out a David to whom he can be a Jonathan."[15]

Considering the story of David and Jonathan again, there is much we can take away from this friendship. There are so many aspects of their relationship that a whole book could be written just about them.

Jonathan nurtured a spiritual bond, showed sacrificial love, and offered encouragement and protection while harboring no jealousy.

Having a Jonathan in your life is wonderful and you are so blessed from that relationship. *Being* a Jonathan is a whole other story.

Being a Jonathan is a sacrificial intention you bring to a relationship.

Being a Jonathan starts with joining yourself to the Lord and becoming one spirit with Him (see 1 Corinthians 6:17). It's an attempt to see others as Christ sees them.

"Greater love has no one than this: to lay down one's life for one's friends" (John 15:13).

Our culture says we should only care about our own success and climbing the corporate ladder. But the best way to become more like Jesus is to help someone else succeed!

Through the tough relationship I shared from chapter three, *Friend or Foe*, there was a woman I met through the planning stages that I greatly admired. She had a decade of experience ahead of me and I had so much to gain from her wisdom. She was able to see through the distress and walk above the mire.

That was the relationship that continued after the dust settled.

She believed in me.

She embraced me.

She loved me.

She lifted me up.

She was the polish that buffed the rough edges.

She desired to find a David to whom she could be a Jonathan.

We went on to minister together for nearly ten years. I watched her work, play, and build others up before herself. When our time together came to a close due to a job change, my hope was that she rubbed off on me. The things I once observed now had to be reflected. In so many situations I would find myself asking, *what would so-and-so do?*

Recently, a mutual friend gave me the highest compliment. She said, "When I watch you lead, you remind me of so-and-so."

When two people lean into each other and build into one another's lives, you can't help walking away with a piece of the other.

Therefore encourage one another and build one another up, just as you are doing (1 Thessalonians 5:16).

I have found that you must not only share the Word with others, but you must give yourself as well.

I can so easily get caught up in studying the Word and learning His precepts that days could go by without conversing much with others.

Or we become so caught up in our own little world, there is no room for others to fit into it. This is not good.

Overusing the word *busy* in a relationship will send the message that you don't have time for the other person, and, in return, all that person hears is that you don't care. They feel abandoned and rejected.

Sometimes things that may seem to be an interruption, when assessed, really are beneficial. Will you and I lift our heads to watch for the needs of others? And when we see it, will we act on it?

I desire to have the same longing that Paul had for the Thessalonians.

> *Having so fond an affection for you, we were well-pleased to impart to you not only the gospel of God but also our own lives, because you had become very dear to us* (1 Thessalonians 2:8).

TWEET:
Sometimes things that may seem to be an interruption, when assessed, really are beneficial. #friendshipjourney

We must walk our talk. Give God. Give yourself.

It may not always be in the fashion of a visit but a phone call or the old-fashioned way of communicating by writing a note to that person God puts on your heart. I still love to receive a note in the mail in this age of tweets, texts, and Instagrams. If you are like me, there are so many notes

I have written in my mind. Yes, I think a note more times in a week than I want to confess.

I was encouraged by a delayed note . . .

I had the card bought and there it sat for weeks. I finally wrote the note to my friend and the afternoon she received it, she told me it was just what she needed the day it arrived.

She had told the Lord earlier that morning that she needed encouragement and it came by way of a note.

So the delayed timing was the right timing.

I have been the receiver as well and know the joy that comes from unsealing that envelope and reading a written letter sent with love.

Right there it is. L.O.V.E.

His divine power has granted us everything pertaining to life and godliness and we can be partakers of His divine nature. Take a look at the qualities we can possess when we allow His divine nature to captivate our hearts: moral excellence, knowledge, self-control, perseverance, godliness, brotherly kindness, love. These are the signs of a good friend.

For if these qualities are yours and are increasing, they render you neither useless nor unfruitful in the true knowledge of our Lord Jesus Christ (2 Peter 1:5-8).

Therefore, brethren, be all the more diligent to make certain about His calling and choosing you; for as long as you practice these things, you will never stumble (2 Peter 1:10).

When you see these qualities lived out in yourself or another individual, you have assurance that your faith is a visible reminder of devotion to Him.

L ove

O thers in

V iew of

E ternity

If you and I are able to seek the things above, where Christ is seated at the right hand of God and set our minds on things above, it will help us view the here and now differently.

It will help you live with an eternal perspective.

It will allow you to see others through the lens of Jesus.

Again, reading His Word and allowing it to penetrate your heart will move you into action.

In Mark 4:1-20, you read about the four soils: hard, rocky, thorny, and good. This parable depicts our response to the seed (God's Word) sown and the state of how we receive it. How you and I hear and receive it determines how we live it out.

- Hard soil = no response to the word sown.
- Rocky soil = emotional response to the word sown.
- Thorny soil = worldly response to the word sown.
- Good soil = fruitful response to the word sown.

We measure everything that we hear. When I hear the Word regarding my situation, I determine whether it is received or not, and to what level it is received. I measure everything that I hear.

The Word of God responds to my measuring device.

*"The way 'you' hear it, the way 'you' measure and respond
to it is the measure that it works in your life"* (Mark 4:24).

God is not measuring this for you. The man from Mark 4:20 received thirty-fold because that is what he heard and responded to.[16] Another man got sixty because that is what he heard and responded to.

We must remember that apart from Him we can do nothing. We must stay connected to the vine, because it is the vine that produces the power, not the branches (John 15).

What do you and I need to do to live in the hundredfold (fullest potential)?

*"And those are the ones on whom seed was sown on the good
soil; and they hear the word and accept it and bear fruit, thirty,
sixty, and a hundredfold"* (Mark 4:20).

What and who determines if you bear thirty, sixty, or hundredfold fruit?

While reading through chapter four of the Gospel of Mark, I found myself asking multiple questions.

Do my actions represent my beliefs?
What does my life produce?
Just how good is the good soil of my heart?

For so long, I seemed to be under the impression that God determined the percentage of the fruit borne in my life. Yes, to an extent He does, because all things are filtered through His hands and He blesses obedience, but the way you hear and receive His Word will measure the *fold* outcome.

It is the responsibility of you and me, the hearer, to move out of the thirty-fold realm into the hundredfold.

So, as you spend time with God, hear His Word, and respond to what He is asking you to do, will you move out with full potential to bless another person's life?

Will you be the friend to that person He is asking you to be?

Before we close out this chapter, there is one person we cannot overlook when considering the actions of a good friend.

His name is Barnabas. You first met him in chapter four, *What Now? Move On!*

Now Joseph, a Levite of Cyprian birth, who was also called Barnabas by the apostles (which translated means Son of Encouragement), and who owned a tract of land, sold it and brought the money and laid it at the apostles' feet (Acts 4:36-37).

Barnabas = Encourager.

The apostles *called* him Barnabas. Barnabas was not his birth name, but his given name.

Why?

Well, we see him living out his internal belief system and love for God's work when Scripture tells us he sold his land and gave the money to the apostles.

He lived a hundred*fold* life.

Barnabas was a friend to all the apostles, but one stood out in particular: Paul.

After Paul's conversion on the road to Damascus (Acts 9), Paul went to Arabia for three years (see Galatians 1:15-18). When he returned to Jerusalem, the disciples were afraid to associate with him, only remembering who he had previously been — Saul, the persecutor of the Christian church.

Barnabas was willing to accept Paul as a friend and student (see Acts 9:26-30).

He took Paul, who was completely disconnected from the other apostles, and persuaded them to recognize him. He later found Paul in Tarsus and personally recruited him for the work in Antioch, where he could develop his teaching and leadership skills.

In the early years of their partnership, we see them addressed as "Barnabas and Paul," but as time went on they became known as "Paul and Barnabas" (see Acts 13:42).

Paul was no longer the student, but the leader. Barnabas, once the trailblazer, became the nurturer.

Lastly, while on the missionary journey from Antioch, Barnabas had the wisdom to know when Paul's gifts and abilities had exceeded his own in certain areas, and he allowed

Paul to shine to the glory of God instead of keeping him down to maintain his own prominence.

While we easily recall what Paul has meant to the church, we rarely recognize that Barnabas was instrumental in his rise to prominence and influence.

From chapter four, we remember that Paul and Barnabas had an argument, which separated them from working together (see Acts 15:39). However, it should also be remembered that these two men spent many years together as friends and partners in ministry.

Who is God asking you and me to be a Barnabas to?

An encourager.

A nurturer.

A partner.

Later, we see Paul take all he learned from Barnabas and pour into the young Timothy.

This is what it is all about.

Learning.

Living.

Giving.

Chapter Seven

Seasons of Friendships

There are three types of friends: Friends for a reason, friends for a season and friends for a lifetime. ~ Ziad Abdelnour

Living my whole life in the Northeast, I have had the opportunity to experience the dreariness of winter, the messy thawing of spring and its subsequent blooming of beauty, the warm days and balmy nights of summer, and the breathtaking vividness of fall before winter sets in once again.

Living in a climate that changes every few months can resemble the valuable lessons of friendship that each season can teach us.

In winter, though some things die, much is merely dormant and will resurrect in due time. Some friendships are only for a period of time and many years later resurface with stronger fervency than they once had, while others may die to never recur.

Spring can be a messy experience at first, but then the flowers bloom and messiness turns to unspeakable beauty and new life.

Other friendships can start off on the wrong foot but turn into a pathway of meaningful care with beauty along the way.

Summer is a time of harvest, a time to enjoy the long days of sunlight.

Several friendships are enjoyed for lengths of time.

Fall is a time to absorb nature's exquisiteness as well as a time to gather and prepare for the approaching winter. These are relationships you have gained much knowledge from and are able to use that wisdom in future relationships.

We can know by experience that each season doesn't have the last word, but rather is a stop along the path to growth and newness of life.

Just as I enjoy the seasons of the Northeast, so can we enjoy the seasons of friendships.

As we have already established, some friendships die (or maybe just lie dormant), some start out messy but evolve into beautiful favor, some are in full bloom, while others are enjoyed for a season.

Ziad Abdelnour tells us, "There are three types of friends: friends for a reason, friends for a season, and friends for a lifetime."

Some friends are with us for a reason (a specific goal or purpose from God).

Some friends are with us for a season (a particular time in His plan).

Very few will walk beside us as our forever friend.

The only true friend you must walk with for a lifetime is Jesus. As you do, you can trust He'll bring friends alongside you for a reason, season, or lifetime in the ways and times that are truly best.

You have had them, friends for a reason.

You have walked this journey with others for a specific end goal. A campaign, an event, a cause or endeavor. You may not have fully chosen the group you were called to journey with, but for one reason or the other you find yourself fully engulfed in doing life together.

This span of time could stretch for a few months to many years.

It is what you do with it that is important. Do you pour into them with intentional commitment or complain with every decision?

A relationship for a reason.

A friendship for a season.

This friend for a season is God's ordained moment in time.

You may have been brought together through volunteering as a classroom mom, a lunch aide, a Sunday school teacher, a part of an organized play group through a mutual friend, or a work opportunity.

It was a lovely season of time, but it ended.

These seasons are looked back upon with a lifetime of memories. Sometimes you wonder why they ended. You thought your friendship was based on more than just your children, but as they grew apart so did your friendship. You hoped it was more than just a job, but after one moved on, so did the relationship.

It's not bad, but it's not what it was.

It's not bad, it's just different.

You either need to accept the new relationship change for what it is worth, or remain wishing for the days of old that you once had while missing the small moments you still could have.

When our daughters were in grade school, I was privileged to be a homeroom mom with two other ladies. One year, we reflected that we were always doing things together in the classroom, but nothing outside the classroom.

We set out to visit every tea room within a fifty-mile radius.

It was such fun to do life together this way. But it was for a season—a short season in the spectrum of life, but one that impacted me greatly.

Due to time, job changes, and life's detours, we are in different states, but that can't take away the time shared, the personal growth, or the "summer" season enjoyed.

I once read this tweet by an unknown author, "If a friendship lasts longer than seven years, psychologists say it will last a lifetime." Wouldn't that be awesome?

As I reflect on this saying, I find it to be true. These friendships may not all look like they once did, but for the most part it is true. This old saying, "Good friends are like stars. You don't always see them, but you know they are there," is a true statement of lifetime friends.

I have friends all over this great country but don't get to see them regularly, although I always know they are there for me. They are a phone call or text away. But I think what has been the most important is to know they pray regularly for me and with me as I reach out.

And even though you may only see them once a year, the time you spend with them is meaningful and impactful. It is enough to get you through until you meet again.

It's what we do with the time we are given.

There is a time for everything. The events of our lives do not randomly happen by chance; God has a purpose behind them.

There is an appointed time for everything. And there is a time for every event under heaven —
A time to give birth and a time to die;
A time to plant and a time to uproot what is planted.
A time to kill and a time to heal;
A time to tear down and a time to build up.
A time to weep and a time to laugh;
A time to mourn and a time to dance.
A time to throw stones and a time to gather stones;
A time to embrace and a time to shun embracing.
A time to search and a time to give up as lost;
A time to keep and a time to throw away.
A time to tear apart and a time to sew together;
A time to be silent and a time to speak.
A time to love and a time to hate;
A time for war and a time for peace.
What profit is there to the worker from that in which he toils? I have seen the task which God has given the sons of men with which to occupy themselves (Ecclesiastes 3:1-10).

Is it possible for you and me to worship God in these differing seasons?

Is it possible to find joy in the midst of your sickness or to find dependency upon Him in the midst of your failing health? Is it possible to be close to God in ever-changing circumstances? If you only thank God in seasons of great health and prosperity, you will not be thanking God very much, because those seasons ebb and flow like the tide. We are to find joy in the midst of each season and in the transition between them. [17]

As I look back on the times/seasons God has allowed in my life, especially the difficulties with my health, I wouldn't wish it on anyone, but I can say looking back, I wouldn't trade it for anything.

The season of difficulty brought growth.

The season of weeping brought healing.

The season of loss brought gratefulness.

The season of silence brought depth.

The season of joy brought blessings.

The season of love brought respect.

God intertwined the emotions, experiences, and friendships to expose my heart and receive His unending love.

And I am so glad I had friends to walk with me through the different seasons. Some friends have walked the full journey with me and others were for a season. No matter what reason or season, they were ordained by God. They stretched me, humbled me, and uplifted me.

A friend loves at all times, and a brother is born for adversity (Proverbs 17:17).

Proverbs 17:17 is a favored verse on friendship.

A friend loves at all times (reasons/seasons).

When you are down, when you have sinned, when you fall, and when you fail, a true friend loves.

When you fail, a friend's love never does.

I believe that God causes certain people to come into our life in particular times of adversity and for distinct reasons.

As the Swedish proverb goes, "A joy shared is doubled, a sorrow shared is halved."

Rejoice with those who rejoice, and weep with those who weep (Romans 12:15).

When joy is shared it is multiplied and celebrated; when sorrow is shared it is divided and deflected.

Do you have a friendship that is "closer than a brother?"

TWEET:
When joy is shared it is multiplied and celebrated; when sorrow is shared it is divided and deflected. #friendshipjourney

Each of us needs at least one Christian friend to whom you can tell your deepest secrets, confess your sins, admit your failures and fears.

Someone with whom you can be completely open, honest, and transparent.

A friend to pray with and who will keep whatever you reveal to her in strict confidence.

There is nothing more special than having a sister or brother in Christ that is closer than anyone else.

With this friend there is no such thing as oversharing.

Yes, this may take time to establish trust, but it is worth the fight it requires to establish it.

There is such a great need for this today in the church.

It makes the tandem ride smoother.

It knits souls together.

It's a "three-fold" cord that is not easily broken.

Seek one out today, if you don't already have one.

As you mature in both age and in Christ, you will become more aware and watchful of relationships. While observing, you will see who Christ wants you to pour into.

I remember nearing the end of my forties and thinking, *I'd better embrace this whole thing of being the older and wiser woman.* Older is one thing, but wiser is another ball of wax.

I mean, really, turning fifty?

That was my mother.

Oh no, it is me!

How did it happen?

One day at a time, one year at a time.

Most birthdays, I am just thankful God gave me another year, but let me tell you, I was holding onto forty-nine the whole year.

Well, I survived it and the anticipation was worse than the event.

Fifty came and went, and it was just another number.

But it definitely put me into that older/wiser category.

Even though my daughters kept reassuring me, *fifty is the new thirty.*

I have embraced this season of my life and thank God for the new opportunities ahead.

I have some older women in my life that I look up to and always say to them, "You are the reason I want to grow old."

If I can do it with half the grace and love as my "older friends" have, then I say bring it on.

You should always have someone younger than you to encourage, sisters that walk with you in the same season of life, and an older mentor pouring into you.

Pouring into. Pouring with. Pouring over.

This is life on life.

This is living out the Titus 2 mandate.

Older women likewise are to be reverent in their behavior, not malicious gossips nor enslaved to much wine, teaching what is good, so that they may encourage the young women to love their husbands, to love their children, to be sensible, pure, workers at home, kind, being subject to their own husbands, so that the word of God will not be dishonored (Titus 2:3-5).

So this right here, the Titus 2 mandate, is the part that could be frightening about the *"wiser"* aspect.

You don't need to have all the answers or to have lived perfect lives; you only need to have a heart for God, life experiences, and love for people. If you have these characteristics, you can come upon another sister and make a difference in her life.

Yes, you will need to make yourself available, be purposeful, creative at times, a good listener, real, and an example.

But it is all worth the fight.

Recently, while writing this chapter, I visited a church for their Sunday service and the pastor talked about "spiritual bullying." I thought, *wow, there is absolutely no room for that.* There is no room for a knowledge that blows another up, but builds and edifies himself.

As we become the older/wiser woman and live out the Titus 2 mandate, we should desire to shepherd the hearts of those with whom we walk. Tend to their needs before our own.

Just as Christ came to serve and not be served, may He be our ultimate example (see Mark 10:45).

In her book, *Feminine Appeal*, Carolyn Mahaney says, "Our conduct has a direct influence on how people think about the gospel. The world doesn't judge us by our theology; the world judges us by our behavior. People don't necessarily want to know what we believe about the Bible. They want to see if what we believe makes a difference in our lives. Our actions either bring honor to God or misrepresent His Truth."[18]

You will always be His radiance whenever you show love to another because it is His love that is made complete in you.

This will be what attracts another to you.

So, go and shine brightly for Him and make a difference in whatever season of life you are in for any reason. You never know you may make a lifetime friend.

Chapter Eight

Your Husband, Your Friend

You've got a friend in me. ~ Toy Story

STOP! I know your tendency might be to skip this chapter if you're not married, you're divorced, or you're just in a bad relationship.

Please don't!

There is so much more to this chapter than a husband and wife relationship.

There are aspects of this chapter you can apply to any relationship, especially those relationships you may set above your relationship with God.

Just because you are married doesn't always mean your husband is your best friend. You can still be married to your friend, but be best friends with other women.

You can have your cake and eat it, too.

Let me start out by saying my husband, John, and I just celebrated thirty years of marriage. Three decades. I know that is a significant period of time in today's culture with the divorce rate on the rise, but I also know we could have thirty more years in front of us to cultivate our friendship and love.

We dated since I was fourteen years old, a freshman in high school.

Yes, we are high school sweethearts. But through all the different seasons of life, I always had friends. I learned early on in our marriage that he could not fulfill every area of life, nor was it healthy to put that expectation onto him.

Though it is a wonderful thing to be your husband's best friend, I actually don't think that it's necessary for a great marriage — friends, absolutely, but not best friends. In fact, sometimes, putting the expectations of best friends, lovers, and perfect co-parents all in one relationship can end up hurting your marriage by making it seem below average.[19]

Over the years of marriage, raising our daughters, battling illness, career changes, and a lot of conversations, our marriage has become stronger and our friendship more appreciated. I am thankful that I do consider John my best friend.

Yes, it has been because we have made Christ the center of our relationship, but it is also because I have older, wiser women pouring into my life with wisdom greater than my own and I heed their advice.

Through talking with many women over the years, I know some of you live in marriages that are lonely. Lonely for many reasons — maybe unmet needs, but also because of work travel beyond your control. What do you do with that?

I remember when I stepped out in faith to start More of Him Ministries, it meant stepping away from another ministry and what I knew as work for nearly ten years. It meant ending one season of life and starting another. Not everyone went with me.

The friendships were still there, but not the daily and weekly interaction as I knew it.

I found myself working in the calling I felt God led me to, but feeling a little lonely.

How could it be?

My husband was still right next to me.

My friends still nearby.

But still a sense of loneliness.

One summer day, as I sat in my office, gazing through the window at the sun's glare, feeling a little secluded, I realized Christ is my ultimate friend and partner and because my name was written in the Lamb's book of life, I should be content.

It was that simple.

I needed the reminder.

I know it may not fill the personal touch of another, but it is the truth. He is enough.

He is enough when you're the only one in your bed.

He is enough when you cook for one.

He is enough when you walk a trail by yourself.

He is enough when _____. (You fill in the blank.)

God *will* fill that hole in your heart with a sense of fulfillment only He can provide.

Through the years I have learned that a spouse (or a best friend) is not perfect in the ways God is. My earthly husband could not be God in my life and meet all of my emotional needs, as much as he may try. And for that matter, we, as wives cannot be God for our husbands. It goes both ways.

I once read the difference between the way in which human love and divine love affects the soul is, "When we are loved and valued by another person it is like a cup of water being given to our parched souls, but when we realize how loved and valued we are by God it is not just a cupful of water, not even a jugful, but a mighty Niagara that fills and floods the soul."[20]

God has to be our "Husband." God has to be our filling.

And while John does what he can to love me in the way God has called him to, only the Lord Jesus can love me in a way that completes me and will never disappoint me.

> *For your Maker is your husband – the LORD Almighty is his name – the Holy One of Israel is your Redeemer; he is called the God of all the earth* (Isaiah 54:5).

We have to let our husbands off the hook from expecting them to understand our thoughts, predict our actions, and to know what exactly to say when we are feeling a particular way. This is beyond his husbandly role.

This is the role of God.

Although, I must admit, it is nice when they try to fill our love tank. When they do something spontaneous, serve unexpectedly, give abundantly, or respond graciously.

And the same goes for us. They will most likely respond to us the way they are treated.

In Psalm 139, the Psalmist focused on four attributes of God: His knowledge of all things, His presence everywhere, His power in our formation, and His holiness.

You know when I sit and when I rise; you perceive my thoughts from afar. You scrutinize my path and my lying down, and are intimately acquainted with all my ways (Psalm 139:2-3).

God is a personal God who actually knows my thoughts before I think them, my words before I say them, and my actions before I carry them out.

He knows my entire day from the crack of dawn to the closing of my eyes.

On days I feel misunderstood and wish my husband understood me better, I can go to God and know He completely understands the intentions of my heart, mind, and actions.

When I was in that funk of a lonely place after starting my ministry, John and I were driving to church and I blurted out, "Everyone is knitting!"

Talk about a husband trying to read your mind and understand your actions.

He said, "Excuse me?"

"Everyone is knitting."

"Do you want to knit?" he asked.

"No! But all my friends are knitting."

"Jessie, you are called to something different."

It wasn't so much the knitting — it was just that ministry felt different and I needed to accept that and follow God.

One thing John has always been good with is keeping me grounded.

While attending a Bible study, a question was asked: "What is your greatest form of restraint?" My answer was, "My husband."

That is not a disrespectful answer. It is a truthful answer.

John can always tell when I am getting overwhelmed or when I have taken on too much. He is good at pulling me back to see the bigger picture.

Remember the story from chapter three, *Friend or Foe?* When John predicted my resignation from the event I was working on six months prior?

And I didn't listen to him?

I learned a hard lesson of submission, which I never forgot.

When our girls were in elementary school, I was highly involved in the Christian school they attended, which also happened to be our home church. Between the school and the church, I found myself there four out of the five work days. While spending much of my time volunteering (and may I say, I loved it), it was also taking me away from my necessary jobs at home.

I recall John asking me if I had completed a task at home, which he had asked me to do weeks earlier. I responded, "Not yet."

I'll never forget his reply: "It would have been done last week if the school asked you to do it." Ouch!

He was right. I got my priorities mixed up and needed to take a look at what was important. Not only readjust my days, but my attitude.

It is subtle.

It's not always intentional, but it creeps up on you. *Busyness* becomes a distraction, not only with our personal relationships, but our relationship with God.

We can get so busy *doing* for Him, rather than *being* with Him.

We can never allow the *hurried-woman* lifestyle to disturb the relationship of abiding in Him.

A busy life is not necessarily a productive life.

We can lose perspective of what is important when we become too busy doing good things.

I love the NASB version of Psalm 46:10, *"Cease striving and know that I am God; I will be exalted among the nations, I will be exalted in the earth."*

You may know it better as, *Be still and know that I am God* (NIV).

Either words, cease, be still, or *Step out of the traffic! Take a long, loving look at me, your High God* (MSG), they all mean the same thing. SLOW DOWN.

Slow down enough to fit Him into your schedule, beloved.

Give God elbow room to make adjustments in your day.

Making Him your priority will help keep everything else in check.

Carving out the alone time with Jesus helps keep things in perspective.

God first, husband second, family, ministry and so on . . .

*Look carefully then how you walk, not as unwise but as wise,
making the best use of the time, because the days are evil*
(Ephesians 5:15-16).

Time is a resource on loan to us from God. Every plan, priority, and goal should be held against the backdrop of eternity.

Learning to trust God with your time is a challenge for most of us in the fast-paced lifestyle of the twenty-first century.

There are only one thousand, four hundred and forty minutes in a day.

Twenty-four hours.

*So teach us to number our days, that we may present to You
a heart of wisdom* (Psalm 90:12).

Yesterday is gone.

Tomorrow is uncertain

Today is here. May we use it wisely.

I bet if you calculated some of your days, or even just one day, with all the necessary things that need to get done: devotions, grocery shopping, laundry, cooking, cleaning, your job, carpooling, extracurricular activities, sleeping, social media, Sunday school lesson prep, and oh, throw in a visit to the orthodontist and any other appointment, and you could possibly be over twenty-four hours.

We can fill every minute of the day. So when the unexpected comes along, we are easily overwhelmed and unprepared.

For me, building margins of time into my schedule has been a stress reliever.

When I have built margins into my days, I have watched God fill them in the ways He chooses.

You may even need to build margins into your day to be available for your husband.

We all have different priorities and different seasons of life, but one priority remains steadfast.

Seek the Kingdom of God above all else, and live righteously, and he will give you everything you need (Matthew 6:33, KJV).

As a woman, you have influence. It started back in the beginning.

Eve influenced Adam (see Genesis 3:6).

Sarai influenced Abram (see Genesis 16:2).

Rebekah influenced her son, Jacob (see Genesis 27:6-14).

Eve influenced her mate to eat the forbidden fruit. Sarai convinced her husband to lie with another woman, Hagar. Rebekah persuaded her son, Jacob, to trick his father, Isaac.

Women have been speaking to their husbands and sons from the start of time. In all the cases I have mentioned, the influence was negative.

You and I have the power to speak life or death into our husbands' lives.

We have the power to correct and restore spirituality or we have the power to propel further deterioration.

This isn't something that stops with our husbands, but reaches our friends, colleagues, ministry partners, and other family members as well.

You make the choice as to how you will influence others.

Remember, we can be the polish that encourages others to be all God has called them to be; or, if we lack the polish, we can be one who tarnishes the walk of others.

What will it be?

I want to be more like Deborah.

Deborah is one of the heroic women of history. She was one of the most talented women of the Bible—a wife, mother, prophetess, judge, poetess, singer, and political leader.

Her life is a wonderful illustration of the power that womanhood has to influence society for good. The great influence that Deborah possessed is evident in the fact that all Israel came to her for counsel and judgment.[21]

The life of Deborah is recorded in Judges 4 and 5.

A judge's role was to obtain justice for the tribes of Israel in the face of their enemies. Whenever the Lord raised up a judge for them, He was with the judge and saved them out of the hands of their enemies as long as the judge lived; for the Lord had compassion on them as they groaned under those who oppressed and afflicted them. But when the judge died, the people returned to ways even more corrupt than those of their fathers, following other gods and serving and worshiping them (see Judges 2:18-19).

Israel had failed to obey God's rules for life.

It was a vicious cycle. Evil - Judge - Peace. Evil - Judge - Peace. Evil - Judge - Peace.

Deborah was the only female judge.

She was a woman of talent, faith, and respect. She spoke truth, wisdom, and discernment.

She arose to the occasion with grace and power.

Deborah used her tongue to speak God's commands to those who needed encouragement to free themselves from oppression (see Judges 4:6).

She used cheerful, positive words of victory when God's people faced enemies (4:14). Her words were wisely selected and people traveled far to hear her speak (4:5).[22]

Women today, we can imitate Deborah's speech!

As we consider our own influence on our husbands and others, we must be careful to choose our words wisely.

Ask yourself this question, which Oswald Chambers poses in *His Utmost for His Highest,* "Has your life been a good reflection of His reputation?" [23]

May it be our ultimate goal and desire that, by the power of the Holy Spirit, we be *an oak of righteousness, a planting of the Lord for the display of His splendor!* (see Isaiah 61:3).

That we would be strong, stable, and unwavering in our commitment to God and in return, we will speak words of wisdom.

TWEET:
Sometimes words
are not even
necessary, it is just
your presence in
the room that makes
the difference.
#friendshipjourney

Not only is it our words that affect others, but it is our very life and actions that speak volumes.

Sometimes words are not even necessary, it is just your presence in the room that makes the difference. Your life may be the only book someone reads.

By allowing the love of God to be poured into our hearts, we can love others and radiate His joy.

And hope does not disappoint, because the love of God has been poured out within our hearts through the Holy Spirit who was given to us (Romans 5:5).

Chapter Nine
When Daughters (In-Love) Become Friends

When all is said, it is the mother, and the mother only, who is a better citizen than the soldier who fights for his country. The successful mother, the mother who does her part in rearing and training aright the boys and girls who are to be the men and women of the next generation, is of greater use to the community, and occupies, if she only would realize it, a more honorable as well as more important position than any man in it. The mother is the one supreme asset of the national life. She is more important, by far, than the successful statesman, or businessman, or artist, or scientist.
~ President Theodore Roosevelt

A s I sit here, writing this morning among our unfinished game of Mexican Train Dominoes, I can't help but thank God for the Blizzard of 2016.

It was one of my all-time favorite weekends.

Both girls were home.

Sarah, newly married with her husband.

Lauren, home with her boyfriend.

Both arrived Friday night before the storm hit, so we could all be snowed in together.

Snowed in we were.

The fire blazing, a game of Mexican Train Dominoes on the dining room table, a jigsaw puzzle started on the other table, the boys playing their bubble hockey game, plus lots of food and laughter. Oh yes, and shoveling. It sure was nice to have two extra guys around for the record-breaking 31.7 inches of snow that needed to be moved. A little extra cooking, but it was all worth it.

Did I already say, "It goes down in the books as one of my favorite weekends"?

There was a time when all I wanted to be able to do was live long enough to raise my girls. Now I want to enjoy their friendship.

Through my many days of illness, I would wonder if I would ever get to the stage where we are now.

Friends.

Friendship with my daughters came while they were in college. It was such a sweet transition from girls to women.

One that we continue to build on through each new stage.

As I observe my own daughters' relationship, I have watched them go through the years of the younger one idolizing the older one and wanting to be just like her big sister, the roller-coaster ride of teenage-hood to embracing each other as true friends. I would always tell them, "One day you will realize your sister is going to be your best friend."

Although it didn't happen without a few shed tears of heartache as well as tears of joy, in the end, they know they are there for each other and count it a blessing to have a sister.

I have to say, having girls is so much fun! As they have matured into young ladies, we have become the best of friends and even though I longed for a sister, God knew He was going to give me two amazing girls to call girlfriends.

There are lots of positive things about being good friends with your daughters.

I want to be their friend, but not suffocate them with my presence.

It is a hard balance, but one that needs to be established.

I am so thankful for the examples of my own mother and mother-in-law that I have been able to glean from.

Again, it is the whole expectation thing.

As moms, enjoy your daughters' friendship, but allow them to have close friends outside your circle. Encourage their *other* friendships. And don't expect them to share everything with you. This will help keep your relationship healthy.

As our girls were growing up, John and I enjoyed every stage from infant to toddler to school-age and yes, even the teenage years and everything in between.

But I remember a specific scare. One afternoon while driving to pick them up from a sporting event, I was listening to the radio and the radio host asked, "If you had a plan for your kids' dating years, what would it be?"

What? How did this happen? Dating years? I didn't have a plan.

The years fly by.

It seems as though you go from diapers to dorms in the blink of an eye.

I kept telling myself, *don't miss the captured moments along the way.*

One of the hardest words I heard from my doctor through my illness was, "We don't want you to have more children."

I have to admit that was a little hard to swallow when you want more kids. After months of processing that statement, I was encouraged by a friend to not miss the blessings God already gave me. If only focusing on what I did not have was what I continued to do, I would miss the blessings right before my very eyes. Two beautiful, blonde-haired girls needing their mommy. I soon had a heart and attitude adjustment, once again, that changed the way I parented and loved.

I think the best advice I was given as we were rearing our girls was, "You are not meant to be their friends while training and raising them." Friendship will come for another season and time. Befriending your young children can be ineffective because the child is not morally, emotionally, or intellectually prepared to play the role of friend. If you're forty years old and you want a confidante, find another forty-year-old. Find a fifty-year-old.

Find a thirty-five-year old. But don't look for a ten-year-old, a thirteen-year-old or a five-year-old to fulfill that role of friend.[24]

As much as I love my girls and try to show them my love, it is not enough to enable their souls to thrive in the way they were designed. Jesus Christ, and He alone, can provide all they need.

It is your job, as their mother, to point them to Jesus whenever you can.

Through a girlfriend that bullies them.

The rejection from their first boyfriend.

An error on the field that cost the game.

Hurtful words by another.

The loss of a beloved family pet.

You name it, it all points back to Jesus. The starting point as well as the ending point.

Do we get it right all the time?

No. Well, at least I don't.

That's okay. Through mess-ups, bad attitudes, and wrong decisions, your children will see your imperfect life, which can be a building block for a relationship. Being able to say, "I am sorry," and sharing your bloopers with them at the appropriate time and age will show your humanism. It opens up the line of communication for them to be real with you.

You may find yourself reading this chapter and you don't have daughters.

But only sons.

Or maybe you don't have biological children of your own.

You can still be a spiritual mother to your daughters-in-law, your nieces, that girl in your church who needs someone to talk with, that new employee who is looking for guidance, or whoever God brings along your path.

We just need to be watchful.

I know I am focusing on mother/daughter relationships in this chapter, but I also want to address mother/daughter-in-law relationships, too.

I have a dear friend who had only boys.

My family always said, "She raised her boys to be good husbands."

I recently asked her to share her secret with me about raising boys and befriending her sons' other women in their lives.

As I read her response, I thought to myself, *this can go for anyone of us who find ourselves in the In-Law stage.*

First and foremost, the most important piece of armor is prayer (see Ephesians 6:18).

Begin praying as early as possible and try to be consistent with your prayers for your child's spouse-to-be. Even if you started praying for them later rather than sooner, you started.

And, for those of you for which this may be a new concept, just start!

Once she is a part of your life, continue to pray every day for her (and tell her you do so!).

My friend realized her friendship with her daughters-*in-love* is very important; if she didn't maintain a good relationship with them, she would not see her sons and may not have much opportunity to be with any children they may have.

Once our son or daughter's significant other enters the scene, we should desire to have the attitude spoken of in Scripture.

Do nothing from selfishness or empty conceit, but with humility of mind regard one another as more important than yourselves; do not merely look out for your own personal interests, but also for the interests of others (Philippians 2:3-4).

Is this attitude always convenient?

No, but it will be worth it in the long run.

Here are just a few things to consider when befriending your son's other woman.

Be welcoming. Make her favorite foods. Go out of your way to make her feel at home.

Give her permission to call you by your first name (not Mrs. ----)! Tell her that she doesn't have to call you Mom, unless she is comfortable with that.

Be very quick to listen and very, very slow to give advice (especially unsolicited advice)!

Don't overcall . . . try not to be intrusive or pesky. Never stop by their home unannounced; always call ahead.

Keep confidences.

Don't be critical of them; don't criticize them either to their face or behind their backs — or even in your heart!

Be loyal to your daughter-in-love; don't gossip or overshare about her to others.

Resist the urge to take over when you are in their home or with the grandkids . . . *they are in charge, not you!*

Jump in any time you are asked or invited to do something with her; to the extent of putting your own things/your own schedule aside; these opportunities do not always come, so make the most of them.

Write her notes of encouragement and verbally tell her how much she means to you, what a good wife she is to your son, how blessed you are to have her in your life, and so on.

I will end with this little story she shared with me: early in her boys' marriages, they had a birthday party for the boys and she overheard the boys complaining to each other, "Mom likes the girls better than she likes us!" Obviously that wasn't and isn't true, but she made sure the girls knew that they have a special place in her heart and they are her daughters!

Not only is my beloved friend a wonderful mother-in-love, but equally, a supportive daughter and daughter-in-law.

I aspire to be this type of woman and to hear the words from Ruth to be spoken:

> *Then he said, "May you be blessed of the Lord, my daughter. You have shown your last kindness to be better than the first . . . Now, my daughter, do not fear. I will do for you whatever you ask, for all my people in the city know that you are a woman of excellence* (Ruth 3:10-11).

Mothers and their children are very prevalent throughout Scripture, but one passage that has always spoken to me is in Timothy's second epistle.

For I am mindful of the sincere faith within you, which first

dwelt in your grandmother Lois and your mother Eunice,
and I am sure that it is in you as well (2 Timothy 1:5).

One of life's greatest blessings is to have a godly mother. And, thus, one of the greatest gifts you can give your children is to be a godly mother.

The Apostle Paul's preaching may have been used by God to bring Timothy to his actual conversion, but behind his preaching were years of godly influence by Timothy's grandmother and mother.

You, however, continue in the things you have learned and become convinced of, knowing from whom you have learned them, and that from childhood you have known the sacred writings which are able to give you the wisdom that leads to salvation through faith which is in Christ Jesus (2 Timothy 3:14-15).

Having a sincere faith doesn't imply perfection. But it does imply reality with God.

Such faith dwelt in these women; it was at home in them, a comfortable, everyday sort of thing. Sincere faith means that you have sincerely believed in Jesus Christ as your Savior and Lord. It means that you walk in reality with Christ each day, spending time in His Word and in prayer. It means that you confront yourself with Scripture and judge your sin on the thought level. It means that when you do sin against a family member, you ask their forgiveness and seek to work on your weak areas. It means that you develop godly character qualities and attitudes of submission, thankfulness, and joy in the Lord. Your kids will realize that, while Mom isn't perfect, she does walk with God.

Not only are godly mothers women of sincere faith, but also they seek to hand off that faith to their children.[25]

The best way to show your kids your faith is to strive to walk it out daily. No matter if you are in your twenties or thirties establishing a family, in your forties in the throes of walking through teenage years, in your fifties and sixties planning their weddings, or you find yourself in the grandmother stage, we want them to know we *wear our faith on our sleeve* and the difference it makes in our lives. (I do realize these life stages can be at different ages than I have listed but the effect is the same.)

You have heard the saying, *like mother, like daughter.*

But did you know it was scriptural?

Behold, everyone who quotes proverbs will quote this proverb concerning you, saying, "Like mother, like daughter" (Ezekiel 16:44).

Right there it is.

This reference is not flattering by any means, as it refers to the condemnation of Israel and her daughter who would follow her footsteps. But praise God there is restoration available.

As a mother reading this, it is convicting to be careful how we conduct ourselves. Is your lifestyle characteristic of what you would want your daughter to emulate?

As you consider *like mother, like daughter,* your mind can go two ways: As a daughter—do I represent my own mother? Or as the mother—how am I living my life? Is it one my daughter would be proud to refer herself to this saying?

Throughout Scripture we see both the negative and positive side of women. Sometimes, when reading their stories, I feel sorry for those that have been exposed to a tainted lifestyle, all the while knowing I have learned from their mistakes and have no excuse for not knowing God's preference.

Even with that, there are still times we find ourselves in a less desirable situation.

Thanks be to God, that He sent His one and only Son, that whoever believe in Him shall not perish, but have eternal life (see John 3:16) and He has reconciled you in His fleshly body through death, in order to present you before Him holy and blameless and beyond reproach (see Colossians 1:22).

There is a positive woman we can look to with great admiration and view an example of right living. Some may say, "There is no way one woman can be all that."

But I say, we can strive to be the Proverbs 31 woman.

Being a Proverbs 31 woman is not about being perfect. It's about living life with purpose.

She lives a very intentional life. I do not bring her up to make you and me feel less than adequate, but one we can strive toward.

As I read Proverbs 31, there are so many areas in which I have tried to teach my girls as they were growing up. Have I gotten them all right? No, but it's the effort that counts.

She is brave, faithful, a planner, works with vigor, takes care of herself, and her family, is hospitable, observant, diligent, encouraging, she manages and guards her household, all while fearing the Lord.

The most important aspect of this virtuous woman is her spiritual life. She is a godly woman who fears the Lord (see Proverbs 31:30).

TWEET:
Being a Proverbs 31 woman is not about being perfect. It's about living life with purpose. #friendshipjourney

Is your worship a stylish life or a *lifestyle*?

What I mean by that is, do you look the part of a Christian woman, say all the right things and act properly?

Is your life just *stylish*?

Oh yes, it looks good on the outside, while on the inside there is a full-blown battle of rebellion raging.

Or have you made your worship a *lifestyle*, one that seeks the Lord with all your heart, soul, and mind and tries to live it out in every area of your life while taking every thought captive?

The prophet, Haggai, challenges us with this very concept.

Then the word of the LORD came by Haggai the prophet, saying, "Is it time for you yourselves to dwell in your paneled houses while this house lies desolate?" Now therefore, thus says the LORD of hosts, "Consider your ways! You have sown much, but harvest little; you eat, but there is not enough to be satisfied; you drink, but there is not enough to become drunk; you put on clothing, but no one is warm enough; and he who earns, earns wages to put into a purse with holes." Thus says the LORD of hosts, "Consider your ways! Go up to the mountains, bring wood and rebuild the temple, that I may be pleased with it and be glorified," says the LORD (Haggai 1:3-7).

Are you living in luxury (paneled homes), while the house of the Lord is not tended to?

Does your exterior look good, but your heart is dark?

Is your worship a stylish life rather than a lifestyle?

Consider your ways!

Put God first and stuff later.

Daughters. Sons. Daughters-in-law. They are all important relationships. Each one separate from the other, but important.

Our role is to practice righteousness internally and externally in front of our families, so they know we are born of Him (see 1 John 2:29).

Chapter Ten

A Circle of Friends

I cannot even imagine where I would be today were it not for that handful of friends who have given me a heart full of joy. Let's face it, friends make life a lot more fun. ~ Charles Swindoll

When I turned forty, my family threw me a small surprise birthday party.

Surprised, I was.

I only remember pestering (okay, maybe yelling) at my girls for spending too much time on the computer. Little did I know they were working on airline flights for a bigger surprise.

The bigger surprise was they coordinated with one of my best friends to come in from out of town.

When she appeared from the other side of the kitchen, I nearly fell over.

Well, that began a few days of fun and celebration.

The next day we ventured into New York City to see a Broadway play and have dinner in Little Italy.

While waiting in the half-price ticket line at Times Square for nearly an hour, we finally decided to see the play, *Steel Magnolias*. This was one of my friend's favorite movies. I had seen bits and pieces of it before, but not knowing the full story line, I agreed to see this play.

Well, let's just say, there was not a dry eye in the theater.

I recently decided to download the movie and watch it again while John was out of town. Halfway through the movie, I thought, *why do I do this to myself?* With a box of tissues in hand and Murphy and Bella lying by my side, I cried through the whole movie—except for a few good laughs at the '80s hair styles. You gotta love big hair.

Steel Magnolias is the story of a close-knit circle of friends whose lives come together around Truvy's Beauty Parlor in a small parish in modern-day Louisiana.

A relational girl like me loves so much about this movie, but what I love most about it is the spirited portrayal of true-blue friendship among this close-knit circle of friends. They immediately sought one another out during every "moment" in their lives. It was as if they were tethered to one another and were reeled into their circle whenever they needed consolation or celebration.

There are more personal applications from this movie than I can share in this one chapter, but I'll try to hit the major ones with you.

First, friendships are best maintained when you meet regularly with a date on the calendar.

This goes for a circle of one, three, or a large circle of friends.

I know this can be difficult, but as we established in an earlier chapter, keeping margin in our lives is vital for good relationships.

Like *Steel Magnolias,* I have a monthly appointment with my hairdresser and have had it for over eighteen years. We were friends through church and when I was looking for a more local salon, she was there. I have always said to John, "I know the maintenance on my hair is a little expensive, but I have saved you thousands of dollars by not needing to visit a counselor."

Joan Crawford's saying, "I think the most important thing a woman can have next to talent, of course, is her hairdresser." There is a lot of truth to this saying.

Well, at least for me.

She is my senior by many years, a few steps ahead of me with family, life experiences, and relationships. I consider her one of my best friends in and out of the chair. Our monthly appointment is not only about my hair, although Lord knows that is important. It's about life.

She has advised me through many situations, in addition to telling me the truth–even if it was hard to hear. We have cried and laughed together. I always leave her salon uplifted, encouraged, and anticipating our next month's visit.

Some months, we even have a circle of three as another friend follows my appointment. I feel like I am right in the set of the movie.

Like the ladies in *Steel Magnolias,* friends show up to celebrate and to mourn. And in the transition from one part of life to the next, they wait with you.

They give you a safe place to fall apart. They stand with you and listen, not needing to say a word. These friends don't overlook the difficult, but patiently do what they can to help each other laugh through it. There is no such thing as oversharing with these intimate friends; they are vulnerable with one another because they know the benefits of friendship far outweigh the worry of pestering someone.[26]

God has blessed you and me with older, wiser women throughout our lives in and out of different seasons. Also, just some downright wiser women (notice I removed the older) to learn from, be encouraged by, and watch life with.

Women you are able to confide in and share life's journeys.

Women who enjoy pouring into your life.

Women who speak truth into your spirit.

They portray biblical womanhood with dignity and grace.

You may be that woman to another—what a blessed place to be.

I want to be a good apprentice and follow well those who have gone before me.

When I think of these women, Psalm 92:12-15 (emphasis mine) comes to my mind.

> *The righteous* [wo]*man will flourish like the palm tree,*
> [She] *will grow like a cedar in Lebanon.*
> *Planted in the house of the LORD,*
> *They will flourish in the courts of our God.*
> *They will still yield fruit in old age;*
> *They shall be full of sap and very green,*
> *To declare that the LORD is upright;*
> *He is my rock, and there is no unrighteousness in Him.*

These women are of towering beauty, unbended strength; they are steadfast, secure, useful, and they don't allow their age to control their lives, but they let their lives control their age.

We all need a circle of friends like this.

Although, this description is not just for the elderly, but for any stage of life.

We can have friends in our lives that exemplify these characteristics, yet don't have the years to show for it, which can make up a larger circle.

Circles of friends are biblical.

Jesus had different circles.

Jesus was a friend of *one* with His heavenly Father.

Just Jesus and God.

He often withdrew to quiet places (see Matthew 15:23) to be alone with His Father.

While you are alone building your friendship with your heavenly Father, you also befriend yourself.

Friendship with yourself is critical for your relationships with others. You are called to love your neighbor as yourself.

This is the second greatest commandment right after "Love the Lord your God with all your heart, soul and mind" (Mark 12:30-31).

This is the core of who you are, this is your True North. It's your internal compass that guides you through life. Your True North is dictated by the internal strength that comes from the power of the Holy Spirit and Christ who lives in you the hope of glory (see Colossians 1:27).

If you find it difficult to be alone with the One who vies for your attention, you may want to ask yourself, *why?*

Could it be that you are running from something?

Could it be you are desperately trying to hide something from the One who knows the very number of hairs on your head?

Sometimes, we can shy away from our alone time with God because we are afraid of what He will reveal in us.

The sooner you are able to unveil yourself before God and give Him full access to your heart, mind, and soul, the better you will be.

Freedom comes when you are honest before God and yourself. God longs for us to obey Him, not because He wants to ruin our fun or cramp our style, but because He so desperately wants us to walk in a manner worthy of your calling (see Ephesians 4:1).

> *He has told you, O man, what is good; and what the LORD require of you but to do justice, to love kindness, and to walk humbly with your God* (Micah 6:8).

He wants to penetrate any dark place in your heart with His light, a light that will illumine your path.

> *For You light my lamp; The Lord my God illumines my darkness* (Psalm 18:28).

When your relationship is right vertically, it will help you manage your relationship horizontally. Your relationship with God will help open your eyes to relationships with others.

He confided in *three*. Jesus had an inner circle comprised of Peter, James, and John. He took them on special outings and allowed them to witness His greatest glory (see Matthew 17:1-2) and His deepest grief (see Mark 14:33–34). He prayed with

TWEET:
Your relationship with God will help open your eyes to relationships with others.
#friendshipjourney

them (see Luke 9:28) and taught them things He did not teach the others (see Mark 5:37–43). They were His closest friends and confidants. They witnessed more of Jesus' private life than the others.

These friends have the most dramatic influence in your life. They should be people you wholeheartedly trust and who have the same mindset as you.

Having a few of these (good) women in your life is critical to a sane life.

These are women with whom you have built a trust.

Women you can share your deepest longings and hardest secrets with and know they are secure. They love you in spite of yourself. They love you with Jesus' eyes.

There are secrets for a few, while there are secrets for an audience of One, Jesus.

You have to determine what God wants you to share with others or just keep between you and Him. There are times God only wants to reveal something to you that is meant for your eyes and ears only. Stay close to Him, so you know the things to share or keep to yourself.

He trained the *twelve.* He chose the twelve disciples to be "with Him" and share in His daily life. He taught them and gave them assignments (see Mark 3:14-15).

Because of this, He entrusted them with *power* to do the work He Himself had done. In fact, He promised them that they would actually do greater works (see John 14:12–14).

These friends make up an important part of your life.

You pour into each other's lives. It can be anything from your small group, to a team working on an event, to the larger version of *three*. These people are a vital part of your life.

In 2015, More of Him Ministries celebrated five years of ministry. This was a milestone for our team. My circle of twelve from our *SHE Leads* leadership team surprised me with a celebration, which I will remember for a long time. The setting was very intimate with each woman sharing our time of ministry together. The night was a little overwhelming with grateful emotion and excitement for the future ahead. But this is what friends do: encourage, uplift, and support one another.

This team of twelve could also be some of the people God has allowed you to shepherd. It could be the women who are under your leadership.

Your example is one they follow.

That is why having your relationship secure with the One is vital.

Jesus mobilized the *seventy*. Jesus had a close group to whom He gave specific service projects. He sent them out two-by-two (see Luke 10:1).[27]

These friendships can represent our service and church family. People with whom God calls you to work a specific task.

Even though this is a larger group of people, it is a group that will support and love you.

It is a group that can be broken down into smaller groups to accomplish more separate than together. But they always know their starting point.

In Scripture, Moses cries out to the Lord,

I alone am not able to carry all this people, because it is too burdensome for me (Numbers 11:14).

Do you ever feel this way?
Well, there is a solution.

The LORD therefore said to Moses, "Gather for Me seventy men from the elders of Israel, whom you know to be the elders of the people and their officers and bring them to the tent of meeting, and let them take their stand there with you. Then I will come down and speak with you there, and I will take of the Spirit who is upon you, and will put Him upon them; and they shall bear the burden of the people with you, so that you will not bear it all alone (Numbers 11:16-17).

Paul told Timothy to listen to all he taught him and then entrust those same teachings to faithful men who will be able to teach others (see 2 Timothy 2:1-2).

If you are feeling burdened, delegate to those you trust and allow them to take some of the load off your back.

Your load will be lighter, but your team will be stronger as you invest in them, empower them, and entrust them with responsibilities. They will feel more appreciated and productivity will increase.

Lastly, He interacted with the multitudes. Yes, Jesus had a public ministry, occasionally speaking to thousands (see Matthew 5:1). In today's world, these people make up our Facebook friends, our Twitter and Instagram followers and Periscope community. These are people we want to be a witness to and an example of God's power through our changed lives.

You would be wise to monitor this group of friends with what you share and how much you share. It is easy in today's social media-crazed world to overshare and regret it years later, if not minutes later.

If you were to connect the circle of friends I have described, you would see something that resembles a bull's-eye. At the center is the bull's-eye and then rings around the core.

Paul makes this clear when he writes that he desires that our hearts be encouraged so that we:

> . . . *may have the full riches of complete understanding, in order that [we] may know the mystery of God, that is, Christ Himself, in whom are hidden all the treasures of wisdom and knowledge* (Colossians 2:3-3).

When you start with Him at the core (the bullseye) and work outward to the *three*, the *twelve*, the *seventy* and the *multitude*, the core is where it all begins. He will reveal Himself to you as you seek Him in the secret place. He will disclose treasures of wisdom and knowledge beyond your own comprehension, as long as you search for Him with a fervency that drives you to Him and Him alone. And, when you do this, it will affect all other relationships.

Laid flat, this bull's-eye, is actually a series of circles. Like a pebble falling into a body of water, it will start in the middle and then radiate away from you with a ripple effect on the groups represented in this chapter.

Which, in turn, becomes a beautiful circle of friends.

Chapter Eleven

Secret Sisterhood

Friendship isn't about who you have known the longest. It's about who walked into your life, and said, "I am here for you" and proved it. ~ Unknown

The Secret Sisters Ministry was popular when I was a young mom in our church.

It was always so fun to find out who you were assigned to encourage, support, and edify through prayer as well as personal notes, cards, or a small gift every once in awhile.

There was a designated area in the church foyer where you would drop off your package, while being careful to not share your identity, and in return pick your goodies up.

Then the big day came when the unveiling of who your secret sister was at the annual Christmas banquet. It was a great night of celebration and then you would repeat the process for the following year.

Honestly, if it stayed a secret throughout the whole year it was a miracle. Many women would suspect others but still go along with the fun.

There were two women in the New Testament that I always considered secret sisters. You probably know them well.

They are a vital part of the Christmas story. They are Mary and Elizabeth from the first chapter of Luke. Sisters in the Lord and cousins to boot.

Elizabeth is a descendant of the priest-line of Aaron. She is the wife of a priest, Zacharias. She became pregnant with John the Baptist and remained secluded for five months.

Mary, as we know, was the favored woman to carry the Son of the Most High, Jesus Christ, the Savior of the world. She was a willing servant who trusted God as she obeyed His call. After she accepted her lot from the angel, Gabriel, Mary proclaimed,

"Yes, I am a servant of the Lord; let this happen to me according to your word" (Luke 1:38).

God was also calling this young woman to leave the comfort zone of her Nazareth home and share the good news with her relative, Elizabeth, who lived in Judah, which could have been eighty to one hundred miles apart. This was no small thing. A three to five day's travel and the first step in her lifelong journey of sharing Jesus Christ with the world.

Scripture does not tell us that Mary mentioned a word of her trip to anyone. It simply tells us she arose and went in a hurry to the hill country, to a city in Judah (see Luke 1:39).

Secret Sisterhood.

Mary, knowing Elizabeth was in her sixth month, arrives at Elizabeth and Zacharias' home and remains with her for three months.

What a greeting Mary received from Elizabeth.

Blessed are you among women, and blessed is the fruit of your womb! (Luke 1:42).

And blessed is she who believed that there would be a fulfillment of what had been spoken to her by the Lord (Luke 1:45).

Now, that is a greeting.

I often wondered if there was a pineapple door knocker at Elizabeth's front door.

I know, you are thinking that is pretty random.

Not really.

Elizabeth displayed such hospitality and friendship with her welcome of Mary into her home and the pineapple traditionally symbolizes "welcome" and hospitality, as well as friendship, generosity, and other forms of social warmth and graciousness.

Appearing on all sorts of décor—from door knockers to quilts—the fruit symbolizes those intangible assets we appreciate in a home: warmth, welcome, friendship, and hospitality.[28]

I remember moving our oldest daughter, Lauren, into her apartment and one of her friends and fellow-movers brought her a pineapple. He said he Googled what represents friendship and a pineapple came up. I was very impressed.

That following Valentine's Day, I bought both my girls an Alex and Ani bracelet with a pineapple on it to represent our established friendship. Every time I wear mine, it reminds me of my love for them and the joy of not only being their mom but their friend.

I am sure you can recall women in your life who are like Elizabeth.

Warm, welcoming, friendly, and hospitable.

Whenever you enter their homes, you feel comfortable and relaxed.

Romans 15:7 encourages us to welcome one another as Christ has welcomed you, for the glory of God.

Then there was Martha—yes, the one who gets a bad rap sometimes from Luke 10—who welcomed Jesus as He entered her small village and made Him feel quite at home (see Luke 10:38).

Martha shouldn't be identified solely with her complaining to Jesus and preoccupation with work. Yes, she once was chastised by Jesus for not having her priorities straight and she took to heart all that Jesus said to her. Later, in John 11, with the miracle of the rising of Lazarus, we see Martha, once again, the one who went out to meet Him (see John 11:20). Martha learned her lesson, showing later she had learned to behold our Lord.

When she came to greet Jesus the second time, she made her statement of belief.

> *Yes, Lord. I have come to believe that you are the Messiah, the Son of God, the one who is coming into the world* (John 11:27).

If Martha had continued her state of busyness without prayer, she could not have come to this act of faith and recognition.

Martha is a woman of care, friendliness, practicality, and hospitality.

As I look back over my life, my memory takes me back to when I was a little girl. Even though my mom and dad owned a business, our home and our home away from home, The Big Star, always had a rotating door with people of all ages coming and going.

My mom has a gift of welcoming people with a lending ear and a welcoming hug.

From a business to busyness, it never stopped her from putting others first. There would be many times people would come in through the back door of our ice cream shop to talk with her as she was flipping a hamburger and, amazingly, she was able to hold a meaningful conversation.

Watching her is where I learned to value friendships.

Back to Mary and Elizabeth.

I often wondered what they talked about during the three months they lived together, building into one another's lives.

Elizabeth, six months ahead of her with child, tending to a household and a husband.

Mary, learning from her cousin the ins and outs of everyday married life.

Did she teach her how to prepare a meal?

Tidy up a small area in the house for a newborn baby?

Love her husband?

I am sure there was a lot of mentoring happening.

Building into each other's life.

Sisters for a journey.

Do you think Mary left before John the Baptist was born or did she experience childbirth first through her cousin-friend-mentor? Scripture does not disclose this, but one can imagine, maybe just maybe, she was there for the delivery.

Secret Sisterhood.

I am sure the discussions were invaluable as Mary reflected on them with each passing month and possibly up to the day of her own delivery.

Having sisters you can share your deepest thoughts with and they still love you the same is precious.

I once had a week of secret sisterhood. It wasn't three months, but it was one of the most inspiring weeks of my life.

Two women selectively brought together through a common bond. We met one time through a national ministry training and then we found ourselves invited to a week of intense Bible teaching.

Behind closed doors, we forged a bond that could not be broken through long hours of discussion and encouragement, with a little retail therapy on the side and some good meals shared.

Even though we live states apart, I know I can call on her for prayer and guidance; knowing what I share with her goes no further than our own ears.

To be able to ask for prayer from your friends is key to relationships.

Having other women you can be vulnerable with and to whom you can humble yourself enough to say, *I need you,* is a gift from God.

On the flip side of this, it is your responsibility to follow up with that friend.

Check in on her. See how she is doing.

To have a friend, *be* a friend.

TWEET:

Having women you are vulnerable with and to whom you can humble yourself enough to say, I need you, is a gift from God. #friendshipjourney

Whatever you do, work heartily, as for the Lord and not for men, knowing that from the Lord you will receive the inheritance as your reward. You are serving the Lord Christ (Colossians 3:23-24).

Not only do we need to work hard in our earthly relationships and establish friendships, but you and I need to have our secret time with God.

That alone place with God will give you the treasures of darkness and hidden wealth of secret places, so that you may know that it is He, the LORD, the God of Israel, who calls you by your name (see Isaiah 45:3).

God gave this promise in Isaiah 45 to the Persian king Cyrus—150 years before he was even born! It refers to Cyrus' conquest of Babylon while Israel was being held captive. A portion of God's prophecy to Cyrus is that He would give him hidden treasures, riches that had been concealed from view.

Through the darkest night of your suffering, in the midst of your deepest pain, there are hidden treasures of darkness that you will miss if you are not searching. God promised to give hidden treasures to Cyrus in order that His reality would be revealed—ultimately that He would be brought glory.

He also will give you hidden treasures as you seek Him in the secret place.

Cyrus did not receive these treasures as a result of his own suffering, but as a result of a divine conquest. Likewise, when we are faced with pain, loss, and disappointment, God desires for us to unearth the valuable lessons that He has in store for us. You are to enter into a "divine conquest" to seek out what He has hidden in the painful season He has allowed.

Finding treasures in the darkness of suffering is more difficult than finding blessings in the abundance of sunshiny days. But the treasures found in times of affliction seem to always be of greater value; they are weighty with meaning and not easily forgotten.

These inspirational nuggets are what help you to keep keepin' on.

He who dwells in the shelter of the Most High will abide in the shadow of the Almighty (Psalm 91:1).

As you set your hearts to seek God in the midst of the darkness, under His shelter and beneath His wings, your trust in Him will be a visible demonstration to others of His reality in your personal life.

Under His wings you will find safety, refuge, delight, and refreshment, stillness in the storm, joy, and power for your weakness.

Your dependence on His grace will allow others to know that He is trustworthy. Responding to the challenge of suffering with a heart of yielded submission will draw those who are watching to the beauty of Christ. In every storm, every trial of affliction, there are hidden treasures waiting to be unearthed.[29]

These treasures are invaluable to your walk with God.

These treasure are invaluable to those around you.

Some treasures, you will need to discern what is just for you and God and others you will need to share out of a burning desire to reveal God's goodness.

Not only does God reveal Himself in the secret place with Him through heartache, devastation, and brokenness, but He also reveals His will for your life.

Have you ever met with Him in the early morning of the dawn or the late night of sleeplessness?

Those times can be the most precious and intimate times where He unfolds His will for your life as you dive deep into His Word.

To this day, still one of the most rewarding times with God, was the neighborhood Bible study I held in our home for eleven years. We had this one inquisitive woman who weekly grew by leaps and bounds, but I would tell her she was cut off from asking questions after 10:00 pm because her questions would keep us going until midnight, long after the hour of our finish time. She would ask the greatest questions, although scholars could not agree on most of them, and I found myself searching for the answers into the wee hours of the morning. As tired as I was, they were some of the richest discoveries I have ever made.

I have to admit it hasn't always been what I wanted to hear when meeting with Him in the secret place, but from experience, I know what a gem I hold in my hands when yielding to His request out of obedience to please Him.

Sometimes, He closes one door to open another, one that surpasses your wildest dreams.

You just need to be willing to allow Him to pen your story.

Chapter Twelve

Accepting Each Other

The reason we struggle with insecurity is because we compare our behind-the-scenes with everyone else's highlight reel. ~ Steven Furtick

Martha and Mary seem to belong together in God's portrait gallery, just as Cain and Abel, Jacob and Esau do.

Many people bracket the two sisters together, comparing and contrasting their respective traits and personalities.

Martha, busy with household chores — Mary, preferring to sit before Jesus for spiritual instruction. Martha, ever active and impulsive — Mary, meditative and quiet. Truly drawn are the characters of these two sisters, Martha usually busy supervising the hospitality of the home, Mary somewhat indifferent to housework, anxious only to seek that which was spiritual.[30]

When Bethany is referred to as *"the village of Mary and her sister, Martha"* (see John 11:1), the implication is that they were both important women in the community and that their home was the chief home in the village.

Knowing Martha from our last chapter, we can be assured of this fact: that whenever Jesus visited her home, she never had any need to apologize for an untidy room, a neglected household, or lack of necessary provisions.

To Martha, her home responsibilities were never a drudgery. She loved her home and was ever ready to entertain.[31]

Both Martha and Mary sat before the Master (see Luke 10:39), but while Mary thought that listening was better, Martha felt that feeding Jesus was just as necessary as waiting upon His Word. Martha's practical service on His behalf was inspired by what she had heard from His lips and was shown by her love for Him.

Jesus recognized that she was working for Him, but reminded her that she was permitting her outward activities to hinder her spiritually and distract her from what was most important.[32]

The conclusion is explained in a practical way for Martha.

> *The Master said, "Martha, dear Martha, you're fussing far too much and getting yourself worked up over nothing. One thing only is essential, and Mary has chosen it — it's the main course, and won't be taken from her"* (Luke 10:40-42, MSG).

Jesus reiterates that sitting at His feet is the main dish, something Martha could relate to with her culinary giftedness.

Upon another visit to Martha and Mary's house, six days before the Passover, they made Jesus dinner together. Martha was serving and Mary took a pound of very expensive perfume and anointed the feet of Jesus in preparation for His burial (see John 12:1-8). There was no complaining at this visit. Each sister did what she did best.

These two sisters in that Bethany family had their respective, appropriate talents, and each of them served the Master accordingly.

And Scripture tell us that Jesus loved Martha and her sister and Lazarus (see John 11:5).

Two women with different gifts found a place very near and dear to Jesus' heart.

Two women with different gifts accepted each other for their individual work.

How many times while working in the kitchen at a church gathering, an event or a hosted labor of love, do you hear women say, "Just call me Martha"?

I know I have said this.

We tend to put each other in two categories of either being a Mary or a Martha.

I truly believe that you and I can find intimacy with God in the busyness of life, and as Joanna Weaver's title implies, you can have a *Mary Heart in a Martha World.*

Will it take some work on your part?

Absolutely, but it will come with a learned balance of when enough is enough and when too much is too much.

The one thing I always appreciate when I am asked to speak at a retreat or conference is to watch the Marthas become Marys when the program begins. They take the hat of organizing off, to replace it with the hat of receiving.

Our family is blessed with the example of my husband's mother, my mother-in-law and our girl's grandmother, to always be welcomed into her home with grace and love. It takes time and effort to prepare for our arrival, yet she always welcomes us with a glorious greeting and makes us feel like we are the only ones that matter. She is able to do this because she has learned to be content in whatever circumstances she finds herself. She knows how to get along with humble means, and she also knows how to live in prosperity; in any and every circumstance she has learned the secret of being filled and going hungry, both of having abundance and suffering need (see Philippians 4:11-12).

I believe if we could embrace this same attitude, we would be able to do all things through Him who strengthens us (see Philippians 4:13).

Don't be too hard on yourself; this could feel like a lifetime endeavor, but I am convinced that we can have small victories along the way.

Appreciating the balance between being a Mary and a Martha is vital to our everyday life, but what equally impacted me about this story is that both sisters came to accept each other for their individual gifts.

Ephesians 4:12 says, the gifts distributed to each person is for the equipping of the saints for the work of service, to the building up of the body of Christ.

So, why then is it difficult for women to be happy for others when they succeed?

Or rejoice with another when watching a sister walk in her giftedness?

I doubt I am going to answer this age-long question in one chapter, but I will try to shed light on accepting each other.

It starts as early as the toddler stage, grasping for the affection of mommy and daddy.

Then you reach the middle years of adolescence and wonder why you are the last one picked for the infamous dodgeball gym game or why you weren't named to the homecoming court.

As you grow into adulthood, so-and-so was asked to lead or the girl in the cubicle next to you was promoted.

You try not to show your disappointment, but it is hard.

When disappointment is allowed to fester into envy, it will bring rottenness to your bones (see Proverbs 14:30).

Disappointment is not a sin. How we handle it is the crucial issue.

Envy is defined as "a feeling of discontent and resentment aroused by another's desirable possessions or qualities, accompanied by a strong desire to have them for oneself." [33] We can go back as far as Genesis 29 and the battle of the brides, Rachel and Leah.

Rachel had what Leah wanted—Jacob's love. But she was jealous of Leah because she wanted what Leah had—children.

And so the contest began for the love and acceptance of the same man.

It ruled both their lives and overtook every move they made.

That is what envy and jealousy will do in your life if you allow it and don't nip it in the bud—it turns into idol worship when wishing you had something the other person has.

It robs you of contentment, peace, and joy.

Oh, we are all guilty of this at one time or the other.

Even if you have won the battle in a particular area, it takes only a split second for someone to walk into the room and insecurity, inadequacy, or feelings of unacceptance flood your soul.

> **TWEET:**
> Jealousy and envy turn into idol worship when wishing you had something the other person has. #friendshipjourney

What do you do with it?

Stuff it down or bring it before the King?

We are to *take every thought captive to obey Christ* (see 2 Corinthians 10:5).

Take heart: as God empowers you to focus your mind on the right things, it will become easier. You *can* develop a new frame of reference, based on what is *true, noble, right, pure, lovely, admirable, excellent,* and *praiseworthy* (see Philippians 4:8).

It is His mighty power in you, all the fullness of the Godhead, that will empower you to fulfill the ministry before you.

We read in the Bible the distribution of different gifts to each person is for the equipping of the saints for the work of service, to the building up of the body of Christ. Each one of us has been given a gift: prophecy, service, teaching, encouragement, leadership, showing mercy, faith, healing, speaking in tongues, etc. All the gifts come under two categories of speaking and service for the glorification of Jesus Christ (see 1 Peter 4:11).

If you walk in the giftedness given to you, and your sister next to you does the same, you could walk side by side, exercising the gift lavished on you.

Embrace your calling and stay in your own lane.

Second Timothy 1:6 tells us to kindle afresh the gift of God which is in you.

Practice your gift, not someone else's.

I want you to know I have not arrived at the whole concept of staying in my lane.

Am I better than I was?

Yes, but I still need to fight the urge to not become discouraged when something doesn't go the way I think it should or I wish I was a little farther ahead than where I am.

Today, social media doesn't help in the category of insecurity. It is one of the biggest culprits to feed our desire for wanting the life of someone else.

A single woman viewing wedding pictures of a girl years younger than her.

A girl showing off a new outfit she tried on, and that is all she did — try it on — but it gives the illusion that she bought it.

Your friend receives flowers on Valentine's day and you receive only a kiss, or have no valentine to even share the day with.

A vacation spent at an exotic island, and all you can do is eat popsicles at the kiddie pool in your backyard.

You get my drift.

I know many women that have fasted from social media for the very reason of the green-eyed monster of envy that evolves when skimming.

Sometimes it isn't even intentional. It's just what the world does now.

If we could just get to where we could be happy for others and encourage them where they are. Uplift them in all that God is doing in and through them, we would be better for it.

If we could just accept our own lot, like Mary in Luke 1:38, *may it be done to me according to your word,* it would be a better place for our families and friends.

There are so many women that think they want someone else's life. It looks perfect on the surface, but do they really want all of it?

Or do they only want what they see in a particular season of life?

How does that saying go—"the grass always looks greener on the other side of the fence"?

You don't always know the story behind a woman's life.

You can't judge a book by its cover.

A dear friend, reading the unedited version of this book, wrote me this insight after reading the preceding paragraph:

"From my experience, every person has challenges, some are more publicly known than others. Those people that have challenges that are known, normally receive more support because it is known. While those who face issues that need to be kept confidential to protect the innocent and for a myriad of other reasons seem to be falsely labeled. I praise God that He knows all things and He calls us to pray, encourage, and support His children even when the situation is not revealed through flesh and blood."

We never know all that someone is going through; and that is why, at times, you need to cut the other person some slack.

All your friend may need are the words spoken, "good job!"

There are women who need to know you notice them.

While observing their efforts, you give them a shout out. The power of applause will go a long way.

- If you observe your fellow sister loving her husband well — Exalt her.
- If you view your grown daughter rearing her children in the admonition of the Lord — Praise her.
- If you witness your ministry partner excelling — Congratulate her.
- If you see growth in your friend within an area you knew she was struggling — Encourage her.
- If you see a younger woman go after her dreams — Support her.
- If you notice a friend's cute outfit — Compliment her.

Practicing wishing others well will help you feel better about yourself and you will brighten another's face.

Fervently love others from your heart (1 Peter 1:22).

One Sunday morning during a church service as the pastor was preaching, I thought to myself, *I hope my friend is listening to this message. It is just for her.*

It wasn't one of those messages you think needs to be heard by a friend because you want the other person to change. No, it was the opposite. It was an uplifting message and it was what I had seen in her over the last month. The light of Jesus shining through her.

So, after the service, I made my way to her and told her that what the Pastor shared that morning was what I saw in her, a light for the world to see. She was shining brightly!

We embraced with tear filled eyes and both walked away encouraged.

Go the extra mile whenever you can; it will change another person's day and life.

Chapter Thirteen

A Love Worth Giving

That those who have purpose for living are those who live purposefully. ~ Victor Frankl

I am sure as you have read the chapters of this book, your head is spinning with faces, places, and situations, which come to your memory. Some of the chapters may have brought up situations you buried for years due to loss or heartache, while others made you smile and reminisce about the good ol' days, or with each chapter came a deeper appreciation for the present days you are given.

With that, we learn from our past, value lessons acquired, and look forward to future friendships.

I have asked myself over and over, *what is at the center of all our relationships?*

I know, I know, you're thinking we hit this in chapter ten, *Circle of Friends*, but there is so much more to it.

Throughout God's Word, we are constantly having to be reminded about His precepts. That is what the book of

Deuteronomy is all about—remembering God's goodness upon the Israelite people.

I just can't seem to get the picture of the bull's-eye out of my mind.

What is the core of our friendships?

I keep coming back to chapter one, *A Girl's Best Friend.*

Our personal relationship with Jesus, the author and perfecter of our faith should be the center of our lives. The apex of our being.

Yes, it all begins with this most important relationship that will affect all other friendships and allow you to love beyond your own abilities.

> *We love, because He first loved us*
> (1 John 4:19).

The secret to loving is receiving!

You give love by first receiving it yourself.

The weight of the love you have received from God will penetrate your heart to pay it forward to others.

You must first receive His love for yourself.

Imitate God, therefore, in everything you do, because you are his dear children. Live a life filled with love, following the example of Christ. He loved us and offered himself as a sacrifice for us, a pleasing aroma to God (Ephesians 5:1-2, NLT).

*Since you are precious in My sight, since you are honored
and I love you* (Isaiah 43:4b).

*How precious also are Your thoughts to me, O God!
How vast is the sum of them!
If I should count them, they would outnumber the sand.
When I awake, I am still with You* (Psalm 139:17-18).

You are His beloved and His desire is toward you (Song of
Solomon 7:10).

So, my precious friend when you fully receive His love,
let the beauty of the Lord rest upon you! (Psalm 90:17).

*For when you look to Him for help, you will be radiant with
joy and no shadow of shame will darken your face* (Psalm
34:5).

It is His love poured into your heart, which is vital to how
you love the other people He has placed in front of you. May
your and my desire be to live near the heart of Jesus.

It is easy to love those that love you, but what about the
difficult and unlovable ones?

I once read years ago, and since then through many personal
field trips, that the difficult people God allows in our lives are like
sandpaper. When God is trying to build your character, He will
often use other people to be the "sandpaper" that smooths down
the rough edges in your personality. I agree wholeheartedly.

You know them — the ones who rub you the wrong way.

The ones who test your Christianity.

The ones who seem to always find fault or question your judgment.

I have to admit it is not easy to be around these types of people, but once I embraced it as a lesson from God, it became a little more palatable.

Are they going to be my best friend?

Probably not; but can I and will I be amicable with them?

Will I be hospitable while in their presence?

This is where a purpose-filled life comes in.

Victor Frankl, a Viennese psychiatrist who was sent to a concentration camp during World War II, said "that those who have purpose for living are those who live purposefully."[34]

What is your purpose for living?

According to the Westminster Shorter Catechism description, it is to glorify God, and to enjoy Him forever.

You and I have a huge purpose to fulfill: *Glorify God!*

Glorify Him in our everyday interactions.

Again, we are not going to get this one right every time, but remember as I said earlier, it is worth trying.

Where do we even start?

I believe the story taken from Luke can help us.

> *Then Jesus answered his thoughts. "Simon," he said to the Pharisee, "I have something to say to you." "Go ahead, Teacher," Simon replied.*

Then Jesus told him this story: "A man loaned money to two people – 500 pieces of silver to one and 50 pieces to the other. But neither of them could repay him, so he kindly forgave them both, canceling their debts. Who do you suppose loved him more after that?" Simon answered, "I suppose the one for whom he canceled the larger debt."

"That's right," Jesus said. Then he turned to the woman and said to Simon, "Look at this woman kneeling here. When I entered your home, you didn't offer me water to wash the dust from my feet, but she has washed them with her tears and wiped them with her hair. You didn't greet me with a kiss, but from the time I first came in, she has not stopped kissing my feet. You neglected the courtesy of olive oil to anoint my head, but she has anointed my feet with rare perfume.

"I tell you, her sins – and they are many – have been forgiven, so she has shown me much love. But a person who is forgiven little shows only little love" (Luke 7:40-47).

Those forgiven much, love much.

Those forgiven little, love little.

This woman from Luke 7 received much forgiveness and the overflowing love she displayed was her natural response to that forgiveness she welcomed from Jesus.

Simon, on the other hand, did not display his gratitude for the realization of his forgiveness. Yes, Simon opened the door to his home for Jesus to dine with him, but the hospitality ended there. Maybe it was just that Simon took Jesus for granted and in return he did nothing to make Jesus feel welcome.

Are you more like the forgiven woman or the meal's host?

Grateful or thankless?

Humbled or prideful?

If I am honest, I find myself, at times, a little like Simon.

I can become complacent with my relationship with Jesus; taking for granted that He is always there for me with little regard of the cross before me.

I want the love that Christ showed on the cross to always be at the forefront of my mind.

I never want to forget that His purpose for coming to this Earth was to reconcile us to Himself by becoming sin on our behalf, so that we might become the righteousness of God in Him (see 1 Corinthians 5:18-21).

When remembering this, it should change our attitude not just toward Jesus, but our brothers and sisters.

So then, while we have opportunity, let us do good to all people, and especially to those who are of the household of the faith (see Galatians 6:10).

Is your life of service a "thank you" for His inexpressibly wonderful salvation?

Oh, I want to align myself more with the woman in the story before us.

I want to love much!

Do you remember when the truth of Jesus' love and forgiveness for you first took root in your life?

It may have been at your conversion or when the reality of His deep affection for you hit you months or even years later.

I vividly remember it in my own life.

It wasn't the night I walked down the church aisle on that hot summer night in 1983 to receive Him as my Savior.

As wonderful as that was, it was a morning, while reading the book of Psalms some years later, that I fully grasped the love of Jesus and the fullness of His sacrifice for me and that is when I made Him Lord of my life.

I committed to putting Him in charge of my life. Making Him Lord.

Talking with Him, walking with Him, rising with Him, *being* with Him.

I started experiencing life in "three's" *not* "two's" . . . like the three-seat tandem bike, it's me, God, and the other person. It's me, God, and the decision before me.

It's you, God, and the other friend. It's you, God, and that *"what do I do next?"* question.

When the reality of His love overtakes you, you will not only have a heart for God, but you will have a heart for people.

Having a heart for people is a good definition of hospitality.

The woman from Luke 7 was more hospitable than the owner of the house.

She wet Jesus' feet with her tears, she didn't cease kissing His feet or anointing Him with perfume, while Simon didn't

TWEET:

When the reality of His love overtakes you, you will not only have a heart for God, but you will have a heart for people. #friendshipjourney even offer Him a respectful greeting or a glass of water. The nameless woman, in heartfelt humility, fulfilled every courtesy Simon had neglected.

Her hospitality started with a spark found in her heart for something greater than her reputation, where Simon needed a little lighting of his own.

Just like the woman depicted in this story, you and I don't have to open the doors of our homes to have a spirit of hospitality.

Although it is such a blessing to have family and friends into your home and the fulfillment of giving yourself to others is rewarding, you can take that same attitude and mood wherever you go.

Your friendly demeanor and grateful attitude can follow you into the grocery store, your children's school, your employment, church, and another friend's home. Your personal care can make someone feel at home and valued in your presence whether on the soccer field or in the church foyer.

It is a love worth giving.

It is a love worth practicing.

It is a love to *"regift."*

Have you ever *"regifted"* a gift given to you?

We all have done it at one time or another.

I am not talking about the gift you were given and have ten more like them in your drawer already.

I am talking about the gift of Jesus.

Your deep devotion to the One who is your life (see Colossians 3:4).

The treasure we carry in our earthen vessels. His surpassing greatness of the power from God that is not from yourself (see 2 Corinthians 4:7).

This is the gift worth giving.

The love of Jesus!

You and I are nothing without it.

His love can and should be the driving force behind all you do.

Because faith, hope and love, abide these three, but the greatest of these is love (1 Corinthians 13:13).

There is an Old Testament woman I want to close this chapter out with who depicts the love of God through her actions. You meet her on the pages of 2 Kings 4:8-37. She probably is not the first person you think of, or for that matter, she may not even be in the top five women you refer to.

She, like the woman from Luke 4, is without a name.

You know her plainly as the Shunammite woman. But there is nothing plain about her.

She is described as a wealthy married woman in the village of Shunem. She had no children. This woman got permission from her husband to set up a guest room for Elisha, acknowledging Elisha as a true prophet and holy man of God.

We find her first, opening her home to Elisha and offering him food.

She was kind and hospitable with no motive, but to bless.

Her love for God made room for His works and people.

Through her discerning spirit, she approached her husband with an idea that he fully embraced.

She summoned him with a request to prepare a room for the man of God who passed by continually.

Together, she and her husband decorated a comfortable dwelling for him to rest while passing through and he stayed in their guest room.

Out of Elisha's deep gratitude for her care, he wanted to know what he could do for her in return.

Her response in 2 Kings 4:13 — *"I'm quite secure."*

NET: *"Nothing, I'm secure and satisfied in my family."*

MSG: *"No, my family takes good care of me."*

NLT: *"shows her contentment."*

We find her being thankful for what God had given her instead of worrying about what she did not have; she was able to enjoy her present blessings to the fullest.

She is a woman of contentment, compassion, and persistence.

It was in pouring out her love to God's prophet that the Shunammite woman received a blessing she did not even ask for.

She is a beautiful display of Matthew 6:21, *for where your treasure is, there your heart will be also.*

Her heart was above her material needs and conveniences, and went straight to the center of putting others before herself.

Some of you reading this chapter live out the treasure you so deeply value.

While others still may need to polish this area a little more.

No matter where you find yourself, God's Word tells us to excel to the practice of loving others.

We can never out-give or out-love God.

Now as to the love of the brethren, you have no need for anyone to write to you, for you yourselves are taught by God to love one another; for indeed you do practice it toward all the brethren who are in all Macedonia. But we urge you, brethren, to excel still more (1 Thessalonians 4:9-10).

His love is a love worth giving.

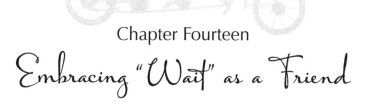

Chapter Fourteen

Embracing "Wait" as a Friend

Success is where preparation opportunity meet.
~ Bobby Unser

Wait. If you're honest with yourself, wait isn't a word many of us like or, for that matter, even accept. Most times we consider it a foe, not a friend.

There are times we run ahead of God when He has asked us to wait and we quickly learn that hindsight is 20/20 vision.

You have heard the sayings: *For such a time is this. Those who wait upon the Lord will renew their strength. In due time, my child, in due time.*

But you want it now.

I am not going to sugarcoat it. Waiting is hard.

A five-year-old pesters her mother for the first day of kindergarten.

A teenager can hardly wait until her first date.

A bride anxiously awaits her wedding day.

A family weathers through nine months for the first grandbaby to be born.

You wait patiently for the phone to ring with that job opportunity you have longed for.

You wait for the results from a recent scan.

A mother anticipates the days when she and her daughter become friends.

It seems, all we do is hurry up and wait.

It is hard to accept waiting.

When you are always hoping for the next season, you tend to miss God in the here and now.

I wanted to include this chapter because *wait* is a friend I have learned to embrace.

TWEET:
When you are always hoping for the next season, you tend to miss God in the here and now.
#friendshipjourney

It has not always been easy, but I have acquired an appreciation for waiting.

Let me share God's perfect timing with you through a learned lesson from my life.

I hope this personal story encourages you to know that God sees the bigger picture and His timing *is* always right.

Part of this is an excerpt from my book, *Road Trip.*

In 1996, while sitting in the audience listening to the speakers at a Women of Faith event in my hometown, the words of a counselor who cared for me in a psychiatric hospital for three months ran through my mind: *"Someday you will be sharing your experience with others."* It was at that event I felt God calling me into a teaching/speaking ministry. I didn't share this with anyone but my mother-in-law who attended the conference with me. Even during my battle with Cushing's syndrome, I knew there was more to life than "just" surviving. I felt that God may use my story in a way that would encourage others. At the time it was hard to understand God's will in it all, and even when I felt God's call, I didn't know what it was going to look like. Yet I still trusted Him with the outcome . . . or did I? Although I felt God's call on my life in 1996, it was a twelve-year wait until I received my first invitation to share at another church. Honestly, there were times I wondered *why. Why God, have You not opened the door yet?* But during the twelve-year preparation, I would feverishly immerse myself in God's Word through multiple Bible studies, as well as work in various ministries. Each experience built on the previous one and prepared me for the open door God called me to enter years later. There were times I felt discouraged that God didn't move a little faster in the process. I wanted to hurry Him along. But through a tough lesson, God wanted me to be willing to speak to one woman, not a multitude of women. You see, what God wanted and what I thought were very different. Humbled by a song I was listening to while waiting to pick up my then-preschooler, God spoke to my heart, "Are you willing to speak to one person?"

When I finally bent my knee to His plan and became willing to speak to that one person, God began His plan, not mine. What

I thought would be a call to reach multitudes, God meant for an audience of one. Likewise, at times you may wonder, *Is this what God wants from me?* His calling on my life seemed to take longer to develop than I anticipated. Yet, through the waiting, I came to know God in a deeper way. He showed me more about Himself, and I realized that this preparation time was necessary for this season of my life. If I had stepped ahead of God, it would have been a complete wreck. I would definitely not have been prepared. And now I am walking in the fullness of His calling. I don't always know the next step, but I learned to trust Him and just follow Him in the day that is before me.

Through the years of wait, Isaiah 55:8-11 was marked and highlighted over and over with great anticipation.

For My thoughts are not your thoughts,
Nor are your ways My ways, declares the LORD.
For as the heavens are higher than the earth,
So are My ways higher than your ways
And My thoughts than your thoughts.
For as the rain and the snow come down from heaven,
And do not return there without watering the earth
And making it bear and sprout,
And furnishing seed to the sower and bread to the eater;
So will My word be which goes forth from My mouth;
It will not return to Me empty,
Without accomplishing what I desire,
And without succeeding in the matter for which I sent it
(Isaiah 55:8-11).

What happened in the wait drove me closer to the heart of God and deeper into His Word. The deeper I went, the clearer His will became for each day that He set before me; to obey Him in what He was asking of me for that specific day given me and let Him take care of the next day.

For His Word tells us:

But seek first His kingdom and His righteousness, and all these things will be added to you. So do not worry about tomorrow; for tomorrow will care for itself. Each day has enough trouble of its own (Matthew 6:33-34).

· Just like the life of Joseph from Genesis 37-50 , you may be waiting and hoping for something to take place, but it has not yet come to fruition. Maybe, just maybe, you are not ready. Maybe God is still preparing you and teaching you so that when He does open the door, you will be more prepared.

Most likely, if Joseph had been promoted when he was twenty years old, he might have been proud, domineering, and unsympathetic. If he would have been exalted then, he may have arrogantly thought that it was due to his own superior talents, but instead God knew His perfect timing for the length of stay in Potiphar's house, the cupbearer to recommend him to Pharaoh, and the revealing of his identity to his brothers and father, Jacob.

It is always easier to read about these stories than to live them, because we have their whole picture from the beginning to the end.

Your story, you are still walking.

But people like Abraham, Joseph, Job, Jonah, David, Esther, and others had to actually walk each day blindly while still trusting. That is called faith.

You and I need to walk each day while still trusting.

Through the wait you learn:

Instruction (see Numbers 9:8)

Patience is learned (see Psalm 37:7)

Rescue happens (see Psalm 59:9)

Hope arises (see Psalm 62:5)

Confidence builds (see Micah 7:7)

Rewards given (see Luke 12:37)

Promises fulfilled (see Romans 15:4)

Valuable harvest redeemed (see James 5:7)

These are lessons you may not learn if you don't embrace the wait.

These are lessons sometimes learned in the dark.

Darkness is a time to listen.

When you are in the dark, listen, and God will give you a very precious message.

I will wait to see what the LORD says and how he will answer (Habakkuk 2:1, NLT).

This means stay put and be still until you hear from God.

Hearing from God is critical in knowing when to make the

next move. It may mean stopping your regular activity long enough to be still before Him and focus your thoughts on Him and what He wants to say to you through His written Word, His still small voice, or the confirmation of another sister.

Will you and I be found like Samuel?

Then the LORD came and stood and called as at other times, Samuel! Samuel! And Samuel said, Speak, for Your servant is listening (1 Samuel 3:10).

We show a lack of love and respect for God by the insensitivity of our hearts and minds toward what He says when we don't listen.

Listening is an art in itself.

Oh, but if I knew it was a direct command from God, you say, *I would have listened. I would not have deliberately disobeyed Him.* The problem is you didn't hear Him.

Is the goal of your spiritual life to have such close identification with Jesus Christ that you will always hear God and He will hear you? Are you so united with Him that He may convey His message through the wind, a flower, or another servant of God?

Most times, our hindrance to hearing from God is our attention to other things.[35]

It's just like my good friend shared with me while dining together — she told me that her pre-teen daughter doesn't really listen to her because she is already formulating her response before her mom is finished with what she is saying.

Hmmm. Does that sound a little like our own personal interaction with God at times?

Again, we see the act of resting in His presence is key to hearing from Him.

This is hard for us in today's fast-paced world. We want instant gratification and will do almost anything to have it in our time frame.

As you wait, wait expectantly. Wait with confidence that God will do all that He says He will do.

As I write this chapter and look through my Bible, I see many handwritten notes next to *"wait"* Scriptures with dates and topics next to them. Some answered and others still waiting. Some with tear-stained drops and others with smiley faces next to them.

One in particular stood out to me.

Delight yourself in the LORD;
And He will give you the desires of your heart.
Commit your way to the LORD.
Trust also in Him, and He will do it.
. . . Rest in the Lord; wait patiently for Him to act
(Psalm 37:4-7).

The year was 2013. The topic is John, softball coach. The note etched next to his name is, "God, you know." When you dream big, you need to depend on God.

My husband, John, worked in corporate America for thirty-one years. Twenty of those years, he coached softball for our daughter's little league teams, their travel softball team, yes, even their high school team, and then he was an assistant coach at a Division I college.

During the last six years of his business career, he planned his exodus from his salesman position to full-time coaching. He earned a coaching and bachelor's degree.

And then his big break came, when the university where he was assistant coaching for four years asked him to be the interim coach for the last three weeks of the season. He graciously accepted and then began the application process to become the official head softball coach.

Wait. Wait. Wait.

It was down to a handful of people and then down to three.

The nearly three-month process drew us closer to God and to each other through dedicated prayer, trust, hope, and *wait.*

And so we found ourselves in 2015, walking a road we had not walked before.

Yes, John was named the head softball coach of a Division I university and with great celebration we said goodbye to a past vocation.

Truly in his case, success happened when preparation met opportunity.

But what about the unanswered notations still in your Bible? You wait.

Wait expectantly with great anticipation.

"But," you say, "there is a *No* written next to the notation." I understand. I have a few of them, too. They can be hard to swallow, but I keep coming back to *God knows best.* I know that may seem like a lucid but difficult answer to a wishful dream; yet, if you embrace God's will for your life, it will be easier to swallow.

I still believe when God closes one door, He opens another door better than what you expected. They may not have been your initial plans, but they were always God's plans. You just couldn't see them until He revealed them.

Chapter Fifteen

Celebrate Friendship

Good friends are hard to find, harder to leave and impossible to forget. ~ Unknown

Well, here we are—you and I have reached the final chapter. Before we go any further, I have to share my final encouragement to write this book. For goodness sake, it seems foolish, but I know God works in mysterious ways.

Besides the fact that with each chapter, God gave me what I needed for the project completion—from Scripture to a note of encouragement, a daily devotion, a Facebook post, a Snapple fact, a friend's conversation or through a personal learning curve—there was one thing that stood out to me and it was the clincher to proceed.

One day while scanning Facebook, a post came up to find out your "one word" for the New Year. I typically don't participate in these types of things, but it kept popping up on my feed for days, so I finally gave into the tugging and plugged in my information. The inputted information was hardly any facts beside your name and a couple questions answered. To my amazement, my one word for 2016 was *Friendship.*

Come on! Out of over a million words in the dictionary, *Friendship* was my word.

For such a time as this.

Bam!

It's time to celebrate!

I am forever grateful for my own mother's love and friendship with her example as my first signs of how to be a friend. The memory of my dad's encouragement to be all that I could be. My dear husband's sacrificed days. My sweet daughters' love and friendship and my forever friends that have polished me so that I would reflect Him better.

As I type the last words of this chapter, we celebrate Valentine's Day.

Ironic?

I think not.

One of the most precious gifts I received was a beautiful card from my daughter.

These were her words: "Mom, You've seen a lot of my friends come and go over the years, heard our laughter, listened to the stories, hugged me tight when a friendship didn't last, and that whole time my best friend of all was you. You've always supported me, laughed with me, appreciated me, hoped good things for me, and told me the truth while still comforting my heart. I love you for that. And I want you to know I'm such a lucky girl to have a friend like you."

Sound a little like a Hallmark card?

Well, it was. But it seemed like it was written just for her and me.

I know through the process of writing this book, I have become more aware of my existing valued friendships and the friendships in front of me I am not even aware of yet. It has made me look at my intentions with greater discernment and be more aware of the needs of those around me. I have been convicted to sacrificially give a hand to another, love deeper, and receive more graciously.

With every word typed, so many of my dear friends' and family's faces were before me, which inspired this book into fruition. But it was you, my sister, I have not yet met or briefly conversed with—I have written this for you as well.

You may not have had a name, but you certainly had a face. I could envision you kneeling at the bedside of your child, aimlessly walking the streets, rejoicing with a fellow friend, driving with a van full of women to a retreat, praying with fervency and living with an audacious love for God and others.

I think it is time to celebrate. Celebrate friendship. Celebrate sistering. And most importantly, celebrate that you are a friend of God.

If you keep My commandments, you will abide in My love;
just as I have kept My Father's commandments and abide
in His love. These things I have spoken to you so that My
joy may be in you, and that your joy may be made full. This
is My commandment, that you love one another, just as I

have loved you. Greater love has no one than this, that one lay down his life for his friends. You are My friends if you do what I command you. No longer do I call you slaves, for the slave does not know what his master is doing; but I have called you friends, for all things that I have heard from My Father I have made known to you (John 15:10-15).

Being a friend of God comes with a high price. It starts at the beginning of John 15 through the above verses.

I am the true vine and My Father is the vinedresser . . . Abide in Me and I in you . . . for apart from Me you can do nothing . . . If you abide in me and My words abide in you, ask whatever you wish, and it will be done (John 15:1-7).

Abiding with Him brings us back to the very first chapter, *A Girl's Best Friend.* This relationship has to be secure above all other relationships.

. . . for He is the Way, the Truth and the Life; no one comes to the Father but through Jesus (John 14:6).

Through this relationship, you are given a Helper, the Holy Spirit, who is with you forever, and He discloses Himself to you and will teach you all things and bring to remembrance all that Jesus says to you (see John 14:16-26).

One of my favorite parts of God's heart is His desire to give us amazing gifts.

*Every good gift and every perfect gift is from above, coming
down from the Father of lights with whom there is no
variation or shadow due to change* (James 1:17).

Every good gift you receive comes straight from the heart
of God.

Many of you know my dear friend, Dora. I have written of
her for years in my other books.

She turned 101 this past October. Soon after her birthday,
she began to decline.

I sat at her bedside along with her daughter and a friend. It
was a moment I knew would eventually come, a moment when it
would soon be time to say goodbye for now. But when it actually
came, I became unraveled.

Yes, unraveled but not undone.

I found parts of my heart torn in pieces, knowing there
would always be a missing piece, but there would always be a
bond that would keep us together till the end of time.

It was a moment of gratitude in an hour of darkness.

As soon as we thought her days were coming to an end, she
rebounded.

It was a miracle. Dora, not sure why God did not take her to
be with Him and unite her to her beloved, Sparky, but grateful
for the days we have left with her.

I now sit by her chair, reading her the manuscript of this
book with each visit.

Precious, just precious.

Over the years, Dora graced me with many gifts such as lovely items from her home to visibly remember her by and all she has poured into my life over the past twenty-five-plus years through our monthly visits.

Her example of loving God with all her heart, trusting Him with every area of life, and her contentment in any situation has grown me to be more like Jesus. Even in her days of decline, she still speaks words of encouragement and her attitude of gratitude is what I am most thankful for.

Just as her love for me and so many others is beyond words and a special gift, so greater is our heavenly Father's love for you as He looks for every opportunity to give you His gift.

He desperately wants you to know that you are loved and valued by Him. He so deeply wants you to know that He is not distant from you, but rather is working in your midst to lead you to abundant joy, peace, and life.

You lead me in the path of life; I experience absolute joy in your presence; you always give me sheer delight (Psalm 16:11).

If we could only begin to understand that all we receive in life comes as a gift from our Heavenly Father, then we will begin to look at even the simple things with awe.

This perspective allows us to appreciate the small things in life and the true gift of His presence in our lives.

If we could only grasp His perfect love for us, allow Him to teach us His ways and walk in His truth, we would unite our hearts with His to stand in awe of Him and all He wants for us.

Teach me Your way, O Lord; I will walk in Your truth; Unite my heart to fear Your name (Psalm 86:11).

Our Father is the most generous person in the universe. He loved us so much that He gave us His only begotten Son (see John 3:16), and He continues to love us by giving us the gift of life every day that we live.

So what will you and I do with all that we have read, studied, and promised to accomplish from perusing this book?

Will you love deeper?

Care greater?

Shine brighter?

Encourage genuinely?

Live intently?

Recently, arriving home from our dear friend's son's wedding in Georgia, I reread the edits from my editor for a final look, and I could not help but share my adventure with you. My daughter, Sarah and I were the only two from our family that were able to make the trip and celebrate with our friends. The setting was a storybook picture. A most beautiful spring day on a hundred-acre farm with a little wooden chapel overlooking field upon field. Horses, cattle, goats, and spotted chickens running around along with the beloved family dog. Sarah, primping the mother and the sister of the groom while the excitement built to when the "I do's" were exchanged. It absolutely goes down as one of our favorite couple of days. We said our goodnights to everyone and packed in preparation for our flight the next day. And then the unexpected.

I awoke to illness.

Was it the flu? Food poisoning? All I knew was that I was experiencing the most awful stomach pain.

Sarah and I found ourselves making the two-hour drive back to the airport with a side trip to an emergency room at a local hospital off one of the exits. Needless to say, we missed our scheduled flight. After some tests, X-rays, and medicine I felt better, only to experience a flare-up of a hiatal hernia.

This is not really what I wanted to end my book with—or was it?

Because, you see, it really is not the story of the health issue, but the story of friendship.

Sisters for a Journey.

Our beloved friends of nearly thirty years left their family and friends at the hotel where they were communing together over breakfast and reliving the celebration from the night before to drive over an hour to support Sarah at my bedside. Through the fog of my mental state, when

TWEET:
Friendship, love deeper, care greater, shine brighter, encourage genuinely, live intently.
#friendshipjourney

they walked through the hospital room door, it was like two angels approaching us. Sisters for a Journey.

They loved deeper.

Cared greater.

Shined brighter.

Encouraged genuinely.

Lived intently.

You did not choose Him but He chose you, and appointed you that you would go and bear fruit, and that your fruit would remain, so that whatever you ask of the Father in His name He may give to you. This I command you, that you love one another (John 15:16-17).

Reflective Questions

Chapter One
A Girl's Best Friend

Reflective Questions:

1. Share your earliest memories of a friendship.

2. Read Genesis 5:22–24 and share the significance of this Scripture.

3. Do you enjoy a 365-day walk with God? If not, what needs to change?

4. Do you allow God to lead the *Guidance?*

5. Do you continue down the road a different person because you walked with Him?

Chapter Two
My Forever Friend

Reflective Questions:

1. Share a time when you were aware of your reaction to a situation or friendship and the impact it had. Positive or negative.

2. Share about the women and friendships in your life that have influenced you and how they have shaped you to who you have become.

3. Why do you think your relationship with God has a direct influence on other relationships?

4. Share about a Jonathan and David relationship in your life, if you have one.

5. Is there someone in your life who needs the power of applause or encouragement? What will you do to encourage that person?

6. Have you ever allowed someone to take the position of God? If so, what was the result?

Chapter Three
Friend or Foe?

Reflective Questions:

1. Share if you have ever found yourself doing something for God and not for man.

2. Share what you learned from a time: *what man meant for harm, God meant for good.* Please be general in your story but descriptive in your learning.

3. Who and what seem to sustain you through disappointment, defeat, and frustration?

4. Do you find this saying, *time will heal the hurts,* to be true?

5. After reading this chapter, do you recognize any baggage that stops you from moving forward?

6. Is there a loss you have learned to live with? Share how you were able to accept it.

Chapter Four
Now What? Move On!

Reflective Questions:

1. How thankful are you that one mistake doesn't stop you from being productive?

2. Have you ever had to intervene with "Eudia" or a "Syntyche"? Please be careful not to gossip, but share how you handled the situation.

3. How has 1 Peter 4:8-9, *Above all, keep fervent in your love for one another, because love covers a multitude of sins. Be hospitable to one another without complaint* helped you this week?

4. What part of 1 Corinthians 13:4-7 do you find difficult to practice?

5. Share a story about an act of forgiveness.

Chapter Five
Sistering

Reflective Questions:

1. What comes to your mind when you read the word *sistering?*

2. Share a story that shows *sistering* in action.

3. Will you allow God to work through you to make His body more complete?

4. Is Jesus an integral part of your friendships?

5. What gift may God be asking you to kindle afresh? How are you presently using your gifts?

Chapter Six
Be a Friend to Have a Friend

Reflective Questions:

1. Just for fun, share a canine story with your group.

2. Share how a friend went out of her way for you.

3. How did the quote by Charles Spurgeon hit you? *"Any man can selfishly desire to have a Jonathan; but he is on the right track who desires to find out a David to whom he can be a Jonathan."*

4. How hard is it for you in *"being"* a Jonathan?

5. Share your thoughts on Loving Others in View of Eternity.

6. What soil do you relate to right now in this season of
    your life?

    -   Hard soil = no response to the word sown.

    -   Rocky soil = emotional response to the word
        sown.

    -   Thorny soil = worldly response to the word
        sown.

    -   Good soil = fruitful response to the word
        sown.

7. Have you ever thought about the fold of your life?
    Where do you find yourself, thirty, sixty or one-
    hundred fold? And where do you want to be?

8. As Barnabas was given his name, what would your
    given name be?

Chapter Seven
Seasons of Friendship

Reflective Questions:

1. *There are three types of friends: friends for a reason, friends for a season and friends for a lifetime.* Share a story from one of these styles of friendships.

2. What has someone poured into your life that you would like to emulate in another person's life?

3. Share a story of a friend that is closer than a brother (sister).

4. Are you looking for a mentor? Or do you desire to mentor? *(Be watchful.)*

5. What part of the Titus 2 mandate do you need to work on?

Chapter Eight
Your Husband, Your Friend

Reflective Questions:

1. If you are married, share with the group how your friendship with your husband has grown.

2. Do you ever battle loneliness? If so, what do you do? Who do you turn to?

3. What is your greatest restraint?

4. What do you try to accomplish in a twenty-four-hour period?

5. Do you agree that women have great influence on men and can use it for bad as well as good?

Chapter Nine
When Daughters *(In-Love)* Become Friends

Reflective Questions:

1. What stage do you find yourself in with your children?

2. Share a favorite time with your kids. Explain why.

3. If you don't have children of your own, who has God brought into your life for you to encourage?

4. If you have had a good role model (mother, grandmother, aunt, or close friend), share what you desire to emulate from their lives.

5. Do you consider the saying, *like mother, like daughter* positive or negative? Explain.

6. Read Proverbs 31:10-31. What aspect of the virtuous woman do you need to work on? What will you do to make the changes in a particular area?

Chapter Ten
A Circle of Friends

Reflective Questions:

1. Just for pure amusement, share a story about this quote from Joan Crawford's saying, I *think the most important thing a woman can have next to talent, of course, is her hairdresser.*

2. Share your experiences with a friend of:
   - *One*
   - *three,*
   - *twelve,*
   - *seventy*
   - *multitude.*

3. Do you feel like Moses when he cried out to the Lord, *I alone am not able to carry all this people, because it is too burdensome for me.* If yes, what will you do to lighten your load?

4. Is Jesus the core of your bull's-eye?

Chapter Eleven
Secret Sisterhood

Reflective Questions:

1. Do you have a secret sister story? If so, please share.

2. Share a time when another woman invited you into her home and you experienced true hospitality.

3. Considering Martha's qualities from the text before you, are the qualities she possesses (care, friendliness, practicality, and hospitality) a part of your personality? Is there an area you need to work on?

4. Can you recall times of suffering when God revealed to you His trustworthiness?

5. What treasures of darkness do you consider hidden wealth?

6. Has God ever revealed something to you in the secret place with Him that you were not fond of? How did you respond?

Chapter Twelve
Accepting Each Other

Reflective Questions:

1. Do you consider yourself a Martha or a Mary?

2. Have you discovered your giftedness?

3. Is there a time when you allowed disappointment to fester into envy? What did you do to rectify it?

4. Share a time when you allowed God to take full reign of your mind and you focused on what was *true, noble, right, pure, lovely, admirable, excellent,* and *praiseworthy* (Philippians 4:8).

5. Share a time when another woman noticed you and spoke life to your dry bones.

Chapter Thirteen
A Love Worth Giving

Reflective Questions:

1. Have you fully opened your heart to God's love?

2. If you have a difficulty receiving God's love, why?

3. Have you ever looked at the people who are like "sandpaper" to you, to be a blessing in your life? If not, how will this change your attitude toward them?

4. Share your thoughts regarding this quote, *that those who have purpose for living are those who live purposefully.*

5. Do you find yourself more like the meal host or the nameless woman from Luke 7:40-47?

6. What do you need to do to be a better *"regifter"*?

Chapter Fourteen
Embracing "Wait" as a Friend

Reflective Questions:

1. Have you found wait to be a friend or foe? Explain.

2. Share a time when the *wait* was worth it.

3. Share a *"God's timing"* story from your life.

4. Do you find yourself in the wait, drawn closer to God or running from Him?

5. Have you found the joy of seeking Him first? *But seek first His kingdom and His righteousness, and all these things will be added to you. So do not worry about tomorrow; for tomorrow will care for itself. Each day has enough trouble of its own* (Matthew 6:33-34).

6. After today's reading, do you think you may still be in the preparation stage of your calling?

Chapter Fifteen
Celebrate Friendship

Reflective Questions:

1. What has reading this book done for you personally?

2. What has reading this book done for your family and friends?

3. Share a story that has happened to you as a result of reading this book.

4. What will you do with all that we have read, studied, and promised to accomplish from perusing this book?

Notes

Chapter One

1. Sorge, Bob. *Secrets of the Secret Place,* Greenwood, Missouri: Oasis House, 2001. 1942.

2. Ibid.

3. "2 Chronicles 15:2b - Our Relationship With God." *ABible.com.* N.p., 01 Sept. 2009. Web. 13 Feb. 2016.

Chapter Two

4. http://www.quotationspage.com/quote/2673.html.

Chapter Three

5. Strong, James. *The New Strong's Exhaustive Concordance of the Bible.* Nashville, TN: Thomas Nelson Publishers, 1990.

6. Ibid.

7. Sorge, Bob. *Secrets of the Secret Place,* Greenwood, Missouri: Oasis House, 2001. 46.

8. Moore, Beth. *Sacred Secrets,* Nashville, TN: LifeWay, 2013. 46.

Chapter Four

9. Jackson, Wayne. "The Separation of Paul and Barnabas." *ChristianCourier.com.* Access date: February 3, 2016. https://www.christiancourier.com/articles/813-separation-of-paul-and-barnabas-the.

Chapter Five

10. ing. *Merriam-Webster.com.* Merriam-Webster, 2011. Web. 8 January 2016.

11. Blackaby, Henry & King, Claude V. *Experiencing God,* Nashville, TN: LifeWay, 1990. 178.

12. The Christian Working Woman (2013) *My Body a Living Sacrifice.* Available at: http://christianworkingwoman.org/topic_content/my%2Bbody%2Ba%2Bliving%2Bsacrifice/ (Accessed: 9 January 2016).

13. McDonald, Gloria. *High Call, High Privilege,* Peabody, MA: Hendrickson Publishers, Inc, 1998. 13.

Chapter Six

14. http://www.quotationspage.com/quote/2673.html.

15. Grady, J. Lee. "6 Qualities of a True Covenant Friend." *Charisma Magazine*. Fire in My Bones, 25 June 2014. Web. 01 Jan. 2016.

16. Edmon, Jerry. "30-60-100 Fold Principle | Jerry Edmon Ministries," 27 Oct. 2010. Web. 16 Jan. 2016.

Chapter Seven

17. Krell, Keith. "Time's Up (Ecclesiastes 3:1-15)." *Bible.org*. THE GOOD LIFE: ECCLESIASTES, 4 June 2008. Web. 16 Jan. 2016.

18. Mahaney, Carolyn. *Feminine Appeal*, Crossway Books, Wheaton, Ill, 2003. 19-20.

Chapter Eight

19. Slattery, Juli. "My Husband Isn't My Best Friend." *Today's Christian Woman*. N.p., Aug. 2015. Web. 14 Apr. 2016.

20. Selwyn Hughes, "Every Day with Jesus," *Alive*, January/February 2016, UK: CWR, 2016.

21. Kachelman, John L. "DEBORAH - Israel's Holy Lady." *DEBORAH - Israel's Holy Lady.* N.p., 1999. Web. 21 Jan. 2016.

22. Ibid.

23. Chambers, Oswald. Daily Readings from *My Utmost for His Highest*. Nashville, TN: T. Nelson, 1993.

Chapter Nine

24. Lehman, James. "Your Child Is Not Your Friend | Empowering Parents." *Empowering Parents*. N.p., Jan. 2016. Web. 01 Feb. 2016.

25. Cole, Steven J. "Lesson 11: The Influence of Godly Mothers." Web log post. *www.bible.org*. N.p., 13 Sept. 2013. Web. 25 Jan. 2016.

Chapter Ten

26. Strong, Kristen. "What Steel Magnolias Can Teach Us About Real Friendship—Chasing Blue Skies." *Chasing Blue Skies*. N.p., 04 Nov. 2014. Web. 01 Feb. 2016.

27. Hyatt, Michael. "The Leadership Strategy of Jesus." *Michael Hyatt*. N.p., 24 Mar. 2010. Web. 30 Jan. 2016.

Chapter Eleven

28. Kaviiks. "What Does the Pineapple Symbolize?" *Home and Garden Decorating Ideas*. N.p., 28 Sept. 2008. Web. 09 Feb. 2016.

29. Wagner, Kimberly. "Day 7: Treasures of Darkness | Revive Our Hearts." *Revive Our Hearts*. N.p., 02 Oct. 2008. Web. 10 Feb. 2016.

Chapter Twelve

30. Lockyer, Herbert, *All the Women of the Bible*. Grand Rapids, Michigan: Zondervan, 1967. 87.

31. BibleGateway. *Martha*. Zondervan, 1988. Web. 11 Feb. 2016.

32. Ibid.

33. The American Heritage Dictionary. Boston: Houghton Mifflin, 1991.

Chapter Thirteen

34. Selwyn Hughes, "Every Day with Jesus: Alive," January/February 2016. UK:CWR, 2016.

Chapter Fourteen

35. Chambers, Oswald. Daily Readings from *My Utmost for His Highest*. Nashville, TN: T. Nelson, 1993.

Meet the Author

Jessie and her husband, John, live in Bethlehem, Pennsylvania, and have been married since 1985. They have two young adult daughters, Lauren and Sarah, and a new son-in-law, Jonathan. Most days, you can find Jessie walking her two golden-doodles, Bella, and Murphy, while supporting John from the bleachers of the college softball field in her most recent role as the "coach's wife."

Jessie is a national speaker, author, leadership trainer, and the founder of More of Him Ministries and *SHE Leads* leadership conference. She also works with LifeWay as their Northeast Simulcast Specialist and frequent presenter at *YOU Lead*. She has a passion to help women experience God's Word for themselves as she encourages you to move into a "wholehearted" lifestyle, devoted fully to God.

The Secret Is Out

Learn it. Live it. Pass it on.

Did you know that God has a secret? One day, while Jessie Seneca was reading Colossians 1:27 in the New Living Translation (NLT), she saw it. There it was, God's secret: "Christ lives in you. This gives you assurance of sharing in His glory." Once you know it, you will never be the same. You can enter into a wholehearted relationship with the supreme and all-sufficient Christ. This study features five weeks of personal, daily assignments and six weekly group sessions with DVD (available separately). As this study guides you into a deeper relationship with your heavenly Father and Savior, Jesus Christ, you will be grounded in the truth of Christ, the person of Christ, and the power of Christ. You will be challenged in your everyday relationships—in the home, workplace, and church. Read and study the short yet compelling and powerful letter of Colossians. When you are finished studying it, you will not only want to learn the secret for yourself, but live it out and pass it on. A companion DVD and audio CD are available for this title.

Road Trip

A personal journey through life's detours and pit stops

Are you "living life" and wondering where all your plans went, only to realize that God's plans were always your plans and you just didn't see it? Road Trip is Jessie's journey in her battle with Cushing's Syndrome, a life-threatening disease. Her story looks back at her ride through the ups and downs of her struggles, how God brought her through them victoriously, and how He is using her experiences for His purposes.

This book encourages you to see God's big picture in your own life and appreciate the detours and pit stops along the way that will help make you stronger and live a more purpose-filled life. *Road Trip* includes a study guide for personal reflection or group discussion.

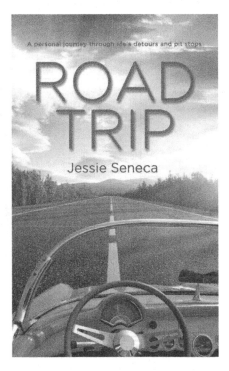

Joseph

A Life of Rejection, Resiliance and Respect

A re you in need of a "pick me up" adjustment? Maybe you have been touched by rejection, shattered dreams, or are presently going through hard times. Studying the life of Joseph will help you understand the relevance of Joseph's experiences—from rejection and hurt to God's sovereignty, every step of the way. As you read and study about this most popular and beloved Bible character, you will find your own place in the journey and see God's plan fulfilled in and through your life. You will come out on the other side with hope, encouragement and compassion. This study features six weeks of personal, daily assignments and seven weekly group sessions with DVD teaching (available separately).

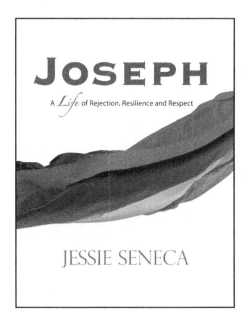

Friendship
Sisters for a Journey

Order Info

For autographed books, bulk order discounts,
or to schedule speaking engagements, contact:

Jessie Seneca
jessie@jessieseneca.com
610.216.2730

To order any of Jessie's books, visit
www.MoreofHimMinistries.org

Also available from your favorite bookstore
Like us on Facebook

Fruitbearer Publishing, LLC
302.856.6649 • FAX 302.856.7742
info@fruitbearer.com
www.fruitbearer.com
P.O. Box 777, Georgetown, DE 19947

Made in the USA
Middletown, DE
15 November 2019

78388577R00119